COMMON
MYSTIC
PRAYER

COMMON
MYSTIC
PRAYER

BY

F<small>R</small>. G<small>ABRIEL</small> D<small>IEFENBACH</small>, O.F.M. C<small>AP</small>.

When thou prayest, go into thy room, and closing thy door, pray to thy Father in secret.."

– Matt. 6:6

Imprimi potest:
FR. EDMUND KRAMER, O. F. M. CAP.,
Minister provincial.

Nihil obstat:
HENRY J. ZOLZER,
Censor.

Imprimatur:
THOMAS H. MCLAUGHLIN,
Bishop of Paterson.
November 14, 1946.

CONTENTS

FOREWORD

"I have found more wisdom in prayer," says St. Thomas, "than in all the books I ever read." How necessary, then, to understand the way of prayer's progress and to advance therein! Much has been written of high states of mystic prayer. Little seems to be said of its humble beginnings. These are so much more common in practice and so ordinary in character, indeed, as generally to escape notice. What is needed, therefore, is to present these imperceptible beginnings in a way helpful both to beginners and to those who guide them. Expansive treatment of the subject is not aimed at here, but rather a brief and simple exposition which is yet sufficient for the understanding of it in theory and practice.

CHAPTER I

PRELIMINARY REMARKS

This book is intended as a simple statement of the beginnings of mystic prayer. It treats of such prayer in its more common manifestations, of its nature, characteristics and effects, in a manner which should be helpful to both the understanding and the practice of it. The aim is especially to encourage those progressing in prayer but unaware of its simple and more unitive forms, and to meet their needs. If the treatment should seem in parts to be deep or complex, this will to some extent be due to the inherent difficulty of explaining an interior operation so simple in itself.

Many are the volumes which unfold the extraordinary and advanced stages of the mystical life but gloss over the simple, obscure beginnings, which, from their common occurrence, are of vastly more practical importance to the generality. Moreover, spiritual writers have given a preponderance of emphasis to sensational and non-essential phenomena such as levitation, voices, visions and the like, thus tending to confuse them in the reader's mind with mystic prayer and to create an erroneous impression of it.

Besides attempting a clear and definite statement of the essence of mystic prayer, it is hoped also to remove unfavorable prejudices and false notions concerning it. Today, when there is so marked an interest, both psychological and religious, in all that pertains to prayer, it is necessary to have an appreciative understanding and grasp of the principles involved in this simplest and most efficacious of all the forms of prayer. Little indeed seems to be known about it. Some even display a seeming contempt or derision at the mere mention of mysticism. This arises from the confusion of mysticism with visions and locutions which would identify mystics with seers and prophets. Occasionally this confusion will manifest itself even in reverent and well-disposed persons. How often people speak of "mystics" meaning thereby recipients of visions and revelations; not distinguishing between these phenomena and real mystic prayer, nor appreciating its inestimable value as compared with all that may be "seen" or "heard" by way of sense impressions.

Again, some busily active and perhaps ascetic person will be heard to say, "Work, effort, devotion to duty," with the implication that this is the whole of the spiritual life. Thus in one breath is dismissed the entire world of the interior – not to mention the ever-present fact that there are souls who hunger and thirst for some more intimate and personal contact with Divinity. External obligations, though of first importance, will scarcely be the *whole* of the spiritual life. Nor can they be held of themselves to satisfy the intense longing of some persons for God.

A spiritual life – if it is to be what its name indicates – must be really spiritual. Where it is so, fidelity to rule and duty is the more thorough. It is a noteworthy fact, more than once pointed out, that where these souls are, and where the interior life is in flower, there above all is found more perfect observance of the commandments and regulations, together with the practice of virtue, love of silence, recollection and spiritual reading. In that excellent old English work *Sancta Sophia* ("Holy Wisdom"), the author, Father Baker, goes so far as to suggest that where spiritual prayer is lacking there is no truly spiritual life. Without subscribing wholly to such a view, one may nevertheless lay strong emphasis on the need of pursuing and cultivating the interior life. When a civilization becomes an excitant to the whole personality and is all aimed to allure the senses to "extro-verted" life, there is need of "introversion," of turning the mind inward to find God in the soul's center. The ever-growing in-terest in mystic prayer, not only of the mere psychologist but – more important – of questing souls, bears witness to that need.

It is by no means to be deemed extraordinary that the Divine Guest of the soul in grace should reveal Himself in a more inti-mate and spiritual manner to that soul if it lovingly seeks Him. The occurrence is not so rare as some suppose. What is rare is a true understanding and appreciation of it. One authority who made investigations in the matter writes that "many good souls, many religious, perhaps most in cloistered orders, have this prayer, or could have it" with proper instruction and direc-tion – if at the same time they possessed a little courage and generosity.

It is not a gift like prophecy or healing given for the benefit of others, but a grace of personal sanctification. Nor is it be-stowed as the crown and reward of a fervent and saintly career. On the contrary, God usually gives it early in the spiritual life and for the direct purpose of fostering holiness, of helping the soul experience more effectually the Divine Life it already has by grace. If the Holy Trinity abides in our hearts, is it not there that we may seek Him with all the strength of our being? It was for this union of love that we were made. The supreme delight of our Heavenly Father is to see in us the life of His only-begot-ten Son emerging in ever richer fulfillment until it has trans-formed us into Him – until the human will becomes one with the Divine and is wholly caught up in love.

The noblest and most fruitful work of man is to develop his interior union with God. It is a continuous process that can go on increasing steadily until death. And nothing can be so pleas-ing to God, as indeed, nothing can be so in conformity with His will, as the desire to advance in this union with Him. Nothing so moves His Heart as to find seeking His Face in prayer and genuine self-denial souls redeemed in the Blood of His Son and destined for the glories of eternal life. And who shall set a boundary to His favors, or say He desires not to raise souls to a loving embrace? If His beloved children sought Him with half the energy they now expend in pursuing mere worldly learning and temporal puerilities, if they strove to nourish the life of Christ in them and to cultivate the Divine Intimacy, they would find a happiness profound and immutable, for they would live by faith, which frees one to taste of the spiritual friendship of Jesus, to live with His life and love with His love – to feel, at times, His very embrace.

"O souls," asks St. John of the Cross,

created for this and called thereto, what are you doing? What are your occupations? Your aim is meanness, and your enjoyments misery. Oh, wretched blindness of the children of Adam, blind to so great a light, and deaf to so clear a voice; you see not that while seeking after greatness and glory, you are miserable and contemptible, ignorant and unworthy of blessings so great.*

Let us know this truth and meditate it for our encouragement and spiritual stimulation: that if we thirst for the Living God, He thirsts for us infinitely more. "And the Spirit and the Bride say, 'Come!'… And let him who thirsts come; and he who wishes, let him receive the water of life freely."† What is this but the Holy Spirit and the Bride-Church imploring the soul to come and taste the water of life? If we make the gift of ourselves to Him He, being God, and acting as God, infinitely, in all His works, will be the more drawn to make the gift of Himself to us. Like the Father of the prodigals that we are, He will come out to meet us and perhaps prepare for us the feast of a more interior prayer – if we seek His Face with all our being.

---

* *Spiritual Canticle,* XXXIX, 7; Lewis translation.
† Apoc. 22:17.

CHAPTER II

ATTITUDES TOWARD PRAYER

Though numerous books are written dealing at least in part with prayer, few seem to assign it a central and supremely important place in the spiritual life. In otherwise excellent religious works there will be a chapter or two on the matter of prayer, treating it as one of many equal sides of a devout life. Rarely is it considered as the integrating force of the spiritual life, the source of its power, inspiration and growth; whose activities, such as mortification, spiritual reading, duties, even sufferings, bear a vital relation to prayer, are ordered to prayer as preparing the ground for it.

An act of self-denial, for instance, made with a view to prayer, will predispose the soul for prayer. It is a step toward the necessary stifling of unruly desires of sense and bringing them under the control of reason and will. This tends to quiet the imagination, encouraging in the powers of the soul a serenity which in turn gives greater facility in finding God and communing with Him. What the soul surrenders out of supernatural love will be recaptured in spiritual compensations according to the dictum: "What is lost to sense is gained to the spirit." On the other hand, one act of self-indulgence will weaken the soul's disposition, will arouse the sense faculties and disturb the inner calm requisite for prayer, especially interior prayer.

So, too, an act of virtue performed in imitation of Christ tends to conform the soul to the spirit of Christ, thus rendering a will-union with Him more perfect and easy at the time of prayer. And indeed, without this life of prayer and union with God, it is scarcely possible to acquire any virtues, for they must thrive on and take their nourishment from it. What determines the measure of a soul's sanctity is the measure of its grace or divine charity. St. Thomas teaches that charity is the form of the virtues, charity then must promote them all. But prayer is the outstanding means of procuring the increase of grace and charity; so growth in prayer-life means growth in charity and divine union. Increase in charity will effect a corresponding increase in the strength of each separate virtue; decrease will mean a corresponding diminution. In this manner the virtues rise or fall with the soul's prayer-life.

Prayer truly holds the central function in the Christian and spiritual life. It is the essential and all-important thing in the soul's progress in God. Not that prayer is to be sought as an end in itself; not even contemplation is to be so pursued. But it is the powerful and delightful means of furthering our one great end – union with the Triune God. It is through contact with God in prayer that the soul imbibes the Divine Holiness. This contact is wrought, not in the senses, but in the depths of the soul, where the Father, Son and Holy Spirit wait to speak to it. Moses after forty days of converse with the hidden God came down from the mountain with a countenance too brilliant to be looked upon. A similar light of grace adorns the soul possessed of a spirit of prayer.

Perhaps it is just this bringing to the fore of the centrality of prayer that is ever needed to balance the scales of spiritual activities. For it is certain that the grace of prayer would render the spiritual life dynamic. We would then regard prayer not as one among many exercises but as that to which all temporal things should be subservient. The spiritual life would be vigorous, with a center of power rescuing it from an all-too-common drabness, raising it again to a keener interest and a new capacity for generating supernatural love and good works. Prayer would be the soul's attraction, refreshment, consolation. Duties, obligations and assignments would lighten under the expansion of prayer and would be considered in relation to it – as means of furthering the union wrought primarily by the prayer-life.

Doubtless it has been the experience of many of us that when we got down to real, sustained effort in the practice of prayer we could note at once effects on our daily life. Contentment was there, a certain satisfaction bringing peace. We perceived an inclination toward recollection, toward carefulness in the practice of little things. The sting was taken out of hardships and humiliations. The initiative in mortifying self and working against it was resumed. But as soon as we began to drift away from that glowing center of prayer, the periphery began to cool in corresponding degree. Surely all falling away from fervent living is due to a falling away in prayer.

So many are discouraged and seem unable to progress. Feeling helpless at meditation, and thinking ecstasy to be the next step in prayer, they lose heart and neglect all further effort as futile. They must be made to know there are simpler, more affective and unitive forms, to which, with good will, instruction and perseverance, they may come. The difficulties they experience may be merely the departure for a real advance in prayer. The certain and fatal mistake is to give up the regular and earnest practice of prayer, for without it there is no holy working of the Spirit.

The people of God should ever be a people of prayer. The special need of the Church today is persons of prayer. A bewildering mass of activities is in vogue, but there is no strong, life-giving substance. Supernatural power is lacking because there is no depth in prayer-life. People of prayer necessarily turn away their hearts and desires from the fleshpots of Egypt and set them toward the Living God. A spirit of prayer makes its possessor unworldly, with a living faith in the reality of the unseen world and the glory thereof.

Is not this the secret of St. Thomas More – of his sanctity, his attractiveness, the impression he made on others? He is generally remembered for his scholarship and heroic martyrdom, but a study of his life reveals him as radically a man of prayer. He attended daily Mass, went on pilgrimages to holy places, and made long meditations on the Passion.

St. Teresa confessed that all her favors and blessings came by way of prayer. This surely refers, not to her many visions of whatever kind, but to the graces of sanctification received through prayerful contact with her Divine Spouse. The gift of mystic prayer in its earliest and ordinary form is greater than the highest natural gift even if that be an intellect like St. Augustine's. It is this prayer which will sanctify the soul and be the channel of the communications of Divine Wisdom.

Let the devout soul take heart again! If it has fallen by the way, let it rise up. Let it not be discouraged and downcast at the seeming futility of years of colorless and routine life, but from this very moment let it begin anew the way of prayer, so that its spiritual life may have center and substance, and abound in interest, power and joy.

What is desired, of course, is the spirit of prayer. This is not the same as merely saying prayers. Very likely persons could be found who recite endless prayer formulas and perform a tiring round of devotions, who imagine they thereby have a spirit of prayer when perhaps they have it not. Others, again, may feel repugnance to such a multiplicity of pious practices yet may have a true spirit of prayer, though they are unconscious of it. It is the constant orientation of the soul toward God that matters. "In praying, do not multiply words as the Gentiles do";* yet you ought always to "pray without ceasing."+ It is a habitual disposition of love toward God in which the human will is ever abandoned to the Divine. This constitutes the true interior life. St. Francis de Sales used to say that prayer is not a work of the

* Matt. 6:7.
+ 1 Thess. 5:17; cf. Luke 18:1.

human mind – it is a special gift of the Holy Spirit raising the soul to union with God. And we may observe that one effect of His operation is an attraction to continual prayer.

"Not many," observes De Caussade, "have this understanding of prayer. Some imagine they can never pray if they do not continually stir their minds, arouse thoughts and feelings, piling prayer on prayer, act on act. They forget the main thing is the attraction of the heart." Prayer is essentially an affair of the heart. "This people honors Me with their lips, but their heart is far from Me," was the touching reproof of God.* And St. Gregory finely says:

> True prayer is not in the sound of the voice, but in the desire of the heart; not our words but our desires give power to our cries in God's hearing. If we ask for eternal life without desiring it from the bottom of our heart, our cry is a silence; but if without speaking we desire it from our heart – our very silence cries out.†

An art is acquired not by mere knowledge of the rules but by the practice thereof. We learn to pray by praying. The Holy Spirit is the chief Guide from within, and He will infallibly lead the docile and fervent soul. He will give it a facility and attraction which the soul must try faithfully to follow. Once we have this taste and facility for prayer – and we can all have it – we are in possession of happiness, power and joy, and the way to holiness and to increasing intimacy with the Divine Guest of our soul.

---

* Matt. 15:8; cf. Isa. 29:13.
† *Moralia in Job;* quoted with permission of B. Herder, from *Christ, the Ideal of the Monk,* by Marmion, p. 357.

CHAPTER III

CULTIVATING PRAYER-LIFE

The centrality of prayer in the Christian and spiritual life may mean many things. It may for instance mean that all is done in the spirit of prayer, every thought and act being directed to God in loving adoration, much in the way of St. Paul's exhortation to do all, even eating and drinking, in the name of the Lord Jesus. This promoting and nourishing of the spirit of prayer leads on to the state further signified by prayer's centrality: namely, a continuous union with God, a life in which God alone is desired, in which the soul is so taken up with Him that it cannot think of nor rest its affection on any object apart from Him.

This is the higher and larger meaning. To live constantly in such union, in a loving remembrance of God which no external occupation can disturb, is to possess the true spirit of prayer. One is then able to converse with God in his heart even while he is exteriorly busy at some particular duty of his state of life.

A mistaken notion is often encountered to the effect that such a life of interior union is incompatible with outward activity. The much too common result is that the search for union with God in prayer is abandoned and the soul is swallowed up in a noisy externalism, the inner life all the while starving for want of nourishment and – in numerous cases – disastrously neglected. This assumption that the inner life cannot be maintained parallel with the activity required by other obligations, is an error. The two can be made compatible. Every saint's life proves it. Indeed, those who have possessed the most dynamic life of interior prayer have invariably accomplished most in the outward and visible works of life. The Curé of Ars, though living in the confessional, never lost his spirit of recollection. St. Felix of Cantalice, begging daily in the streets of Rome the necessary provisions for his brethren, was yet ever praying, his heart and mind lovingly turned toward God. Anna Maria Taigi and Lucie Christine were mothers of families and still they lived in a profound spirit of prayer and union with the Guest of their souls. Our Lord Himself, Who had laid upon His shoulders the heaviest burden of all, carried it perfectly, though absorbed unceasingly in deepest contemplation.

It is just this spirit of prayer and union with God that yields abundant fruit in external labors. Without it, all can easily degenerate into mere natural activity, an outlet for self in one form or other, engaging and important perhaps, but rather ineffectual for building up the kingdom of God in the souls of men or embellishing the crown of personal sanctity and glory for the life to come. It is the life of divine union that is to be stressed. God wants first my sanctification, and if my interior life is hindered, harmed or destroyed by absorbing or irrelevant activity, I am somewhere at fault; I have not learned how to harmonize the two, or I have placed the emphasis on the wrong things. First and foremost is the obligation to search out that perfection which requires us to be perfect as our Heavenly Father is perfect; and this is best done by cultivating the spirit and life of prayer. Moreover, it is only as we really live the life of prayer that the vast graces embedded in the sacramental system are brought to maturity in the soul.

One aid in developing a spirit of prayer is to walk in the Divine Presence. The Christian, made one with Christ in the membership of His Mystical Body, knows himself to be God's child, dependent upon Him at each moment of the day and night. He understands that he is ever loved by his Heavenly Father with an infinite love, that his earthly life is of supreme solicitude to that Father because it is immersed in the life of the only-begotten Son and has a destiny vitally linked to it. The child of God, then, knows himself to be always living under the all-seeing eye of Him Who gives existence to everything, and to Whom he is responsible for all the actions of his life.

For the spiritual man this will mean a consciousness of God, a desire to live in God and to find the adequate prayerful relationship with Him. Accordingly, he will want to cultivate the Divine Presence, will continually contact Him Who beckons him on to a marvelous destiny of everlasting glory; he will lift up his eyes to the heavens and see Who made all these things and drew them in order, form and beauty. Sentiments of praise, wonderment, love and gratitude will well up from his heart before the wisdom, splendor and power of God's creation. Tender emotions of affection will culminate in the longing for a deeper intimacy, a special, close, enduring union with Him Who alone fills the love-hungry heart.

This is a truly helpful part of the preparation for the beginnings of spiritual and interior prayer. The soul that wholeheartedly desires to possess the rich happiness of such a life of interior union will cultivate a sense of the Divine Presence until the consciousness becomes a kind of second nature. To obtain that union will be the first concern of devout and consecrated souls for these are the ones the Father especially seeks to worship Him.

There is no question here of a sensible, a felt, presence of God, but rather of an adverting to Him in mind and heart. In literal truth, of course, we cannot be out of His presence. "Do not I fill heaven and earth?"* He asks. He is present to, and in, all His creation, maintaining it in being by His essence and power:

---

* Jer. 23:24.

Whither shall I go from Thy spirit? Or whither shall I flee from Thy face? If I ascend into heaven, Thou art there; if I descend into hell, Thou art present. If I… dwell in the uttermost parts of the sea: even there also shall Thy hand lead me… And I said: Perhaps darkness shall cover me… But darkness shall not be dark to Thee.*

And this searching omnipresence reaches even to the hidden recesses of the human heart: "Thou hast understood my thoughts from afar off… Thou hast foreseen all my ways… Thy knowledge is become wonderful to me: it is high, and I cannot reach to it."†

So, without and within, to our knowledge and the cries of our heart, God is ever present. But by frequent remembrance of Him – in the beginning at least – and by renewing the single intention of doing all for love of Him, we tend more consciously to live in the Divine Presence. We acquire an awareness of God necessitating, with progress, fewer explicit acts. It becomes a simple spirit of recollection in which mind and heart ever tend toward God, not so much in active advertence as by the relinquishing of all attachments, of divers self-sought and self-imposed activities, in a word, of all that is not God or the manifestation of His Divine Will.

To further one's progress toward this happiest grace of interior union, there is the vastly important matter of meditation. Meditation periods belong to the hour plan of religious life; but this kind of prayer need not be limited to a by-the-clock schedule. The important thing is to meditate. Whenever the mind reflects upon God and the mysteries of our faith or upon the life and Passion of Jesus so that the result is an enkindling of love in the will, inclining it to more perfect service of God, this is the prayer of meditation. It is ruminating over, digesting, loving the truths and beauties of our holy faith so that we are

---

* Ps. 138:7-12.
† Ibid. 3, 4, 6.

moved to correct our faults and advance in love of God and conformity to the life of Jesus.

It may be noted that the essential prayer-element in meditation is not the thought and reflection. This might be a mere mental exercise. Reflection is used to stir the will to love. Only at this point does prayer really begin – when the will is drawn to God in love, adoration, petition, thanksgiving. If little thinking and imagining is required for this, so much the better, for more time is then given to real prayer, the occupation of the heart. It may be that some souls cannot use meditation *as* prayer, as was the case with St. Thérèse of the Child Jesus. For such souls it is necessary, outside of prayer, to reflect upon the mysteries of religion or to do spiritual reading, even as this same saint did in abundance. Without these there is lack of nourishment for mind and heart.

It is surely a damaging mistake to omit reflection on divine truths, to choke it out by multiplicities less essential, to forgo willingly the period set aside or dream it away in idle reverie. Often enough this is the main or even the only opportunity one can get for an audience with God; if it is neglected, the strength for daily progress is not obtained, the day becomes a round of dissipation, and the way of advance to more direct and unitive prayer is abandoned. One may be discouraged from lack of true knowledge of prayer; but again, a sufficient will to advance and learn the way of prayer may also be lacking. The soul desirous of advancing will use the time well and even enrich it by steady spiritual reading.

A third and fundamental preparation for a life of interior union is earnest ascetic practice. Many a promising beginning has come to nothing from feeble ascetic efforts and a failure energetically to reform the desire. "We shall hardly ever see a soul," warns St. John of the Cross,

> negligent in overcoming a single desire, which has not also many other desires arising out of the weakness and imperfection from which the first proceeds. There have been

many persons who had made great progress in detachment and freedom, and who yet, because they gave way, under the pretence of some good – as of society and friendship – to petty attachments, have thereby lost the spirit and sweetness of God, holy solitude, and cheerfulness, and have injured the integrity of this spiritual exercise so as to be unable to stop before all was gone.*

Without a real, sustained effort to mortify sense, to overcome evil tendencies, no true advance in prayer can be made. This effort must include interior mortification which aims at conquering self-love, checking unruly thoughts and affections, weaning the desires from all that is not God. If this is done especially with a view to divine union, God will draw the soul closer to Himself, and perhaps at times even make His presence felt in the soul in spiritual affections. It would be an illusion to aspire to become a person of prayer while at the same time one fostered dissipation of mind and heart, withdrawing them from the direction of God and squandering them on this world's empty diversions. When foreign and extraneous interests are let in, the Holy Spirit is let out. Even restless eagerness for news, under the guise of the necessity of keeping abreast of all that goes on in the world, or comes off the press, easily and surely corrodes the spirit and life of prayer. Such a disposition must be checked if one would find spiritual expansion and the taste of that peace and happiness that comes from rejecting all to find the Spouse Who alone contains all the treasures of wisdom and knowledge. To know the solid truth of this, one need only perform a single act of self-denial. The fruit will be perceived. It may be slight – but it will be there. This kind of knowledge comes only by practice; it belongs to the wisdom of the Cross and the Christian life, and grows with progress in interior friendship with God. "If you know these things, blessed shall you be if you do them."†

* *The Ascent of Mount Carmel*, Bk. I, chap. 2.
† John 13:17.

But there is more. The renunciation is to extend, says St. John of the Cross, even to spiritual things. Some there are who

think it enough to deny themselves in the things of this world without purging away all self-seeking in spiritual things. Hence it comes to pass that when any of this solid devotion presents itself to them which consists in the annihilation of all sweetness in God, in dryness, in distaste, in trouble, which is the real spiritual Cross, and the nakedness of the spiritual poverty of Christ, they run away from it as from death itself. They seek only for delights, for sweet communications and satisfactions in God, but this is not self-denial nor detachment of spirit, but rather spiritual gluttony. They render themselves spiritually enemies of the Cross of Christ, for true spirituality seeks for bitterness rather than sweetness in God, inclines to suffering more than to consolation, and to be in want of everything for God rather than to possess; to dryness and afflictions rather than to sweet communications, knowing well that this is to follow Christ and deny self, while the other course is perhaps nothing but to seek oneself in God, which is the very opposite of love. For to seek self in God is to seek for comfort and refreshment from God. But to seek God in Himself is not only to be willingly deprived of this thing and of that for God, but to incline ourselves to will and choose for Christ's sake whatever is most disagreeable, whether proceeding from God or from the world.*

The virile exhortation of the saints to pursue prayer unrelentingly cannot be echoed too strongly. Nourish the prayer-life with constant self-denial and the virtues of Christ. Fill it with holy reading that will furnish matter for meditation and inspire the Christian soul, the spouse of Christ, to mature its vocation – which is to be a saint of God. It is all imperative – yet simple. The earnest soul will reap its reward, and that quickly. For God is watching it, observing its efforts and the desires of

---

* *The Ascent of Mount Carmel,* Bk. II, chap. 7.

its heart, awaiting the propitious moment to simplify its spiritual life in a prayer of deeper love: a spiritual prayer, requiring little effort on the soul's part, not sensible, but very satisfying, and in its nature mystical.

Always the Divine Lover invites us on to closer union – even to the union of this simple mystic prayer. Many, if they persevered, would surely receive this grace from God. And many do receive it, for which reason it may be designated "common" mystic prayer as distinguished from advanced degrees, which are less usual.

May we desire and pray for such a grace? Undoubtedly! – even as we pray for any other gift of God. To pray for this grace is simply to pray for progress in prayer. It is the traditional teaching of theologians that mystic prayer belongs to the order of grace, is a further development or communication of sanctifying grace. Thus we find St. Bonaventure making it the basis of his mystical doctrine that "the desire of mystical union is not merely a lawful tendency, but a necessary one, in the soul which is fully corresponding with the grace of God."* So, too, a modern theologian, Père Grandmaison, finds not only that the desire for this grace is lawful but that those who wish to correspond fully with the workings of God upon the human soul are bound to have that desire.†

It is the desires of the heart that count with God. Daniel is called by an angel pleasing to the Lord because he is "a man of desires."‡ What is necessary is elevation of the desires to God and loving union with Him. Our Heavenly Father thirsts for such intimacy with His beloved children.

All you that thirst, come to the waters; and you that have no money, make haste, buy and eat; come ye, buy wine and milk without money, and without any price. Why do you spend money for that which is not bread, and your labor for

---

* Dobbins, *Franciscan Mysticism,* pp. 136-137.
† Ibid., p. 138.
‡ Dan. 9:23.

that which doth not satisfy you? Hearken diligently to Me, and eat that which is good, and your soul shall be delighted in fatness.*

So speaks the Holy Spirit by the mouth of Isaias. And centuries later, "Jesus stood and cried out, saying, 'If anyone thirst, let him come to Me and drink.' "†

* Isa. 55:1-2.
† John 7:37.

CHAPTER IV

ON THE USE OF A TERM

It may be surmised that if there is any distrust of mysticism, it is due to a misconception of its real nature. Some who have written on the subject have written from personal experience. Others have written after prolonged study, without perhaps the direct experience. This may account for the opposing judgments, the varying discernments and enthusiasms, found among spiritual authors. One excellent ascetical treatise, for instance, would convey the impression that mystical or contemplative prayer is not linked with the normal course of the supernatural life, bears no direct relation to it, but is wholly extraordinary, eccentric, queer. Such a view has wrought damage by fostering mistaken notions and evoking adverse prejudice. Happily, the idea is now tending to correct itself.

A Catholic philosopher deplores the fact that

mysticism should still be so widely regarded with suspicion even by Catholic writers, as something abnormal, something with which the healthy religion of normal folk has no concern. Or at best it is considered an extraordinary favor, granted like miracle-working to a few chosen souls, with which the ordinary Catholic has nothing to do. Yet mysticism is the very life-blood of sanctity.*

---

* Watkin, *The Bow in the Clouds,* p. 165; by permission of the Macmillan Company.

Mysticism, the same writer goes on to say, is not an accident of religion or something extrinsic to it, but "belongs to the supernatural life of sanctifying grace and is organically connected with it"* This in no way conflicts with the fact that mystic prayer is not attainable solely by one's own effort but remains in the end a gift from God. A new impulse of grace comes in, changing the soul's mode of communication with God, and effecting a purer, more spiritual relationship with Him. It is a blossoming of the Christian supernatural life in this world as the Beatific Vision is its full flowering in the next.

In view of these remarks it is not only desirable but necessary to attach an exact signification to the term "mysticism." The connotations of this word as so carelessly bandied about in daily life are various and vague. In the popular imagination it covers a multitude of oddities. Some identify it with an impractical idealism, labeling one guilty of such idealism a "mystic dreamer." Others associate it mainly with any brand of occultism imported from the East. Often it is used as suggesting mere mental mistiness and confusion of thought. Or again it is exploited in literary criticism, when, for instance, certain poets are called "nature mystics," as seeming to possess a power of intuition in penetrating nature's veil to the hidden meaning of her phenomena.

In the present treatise the term is employed in its most limited, its theological sense, as referring to a very definite religious experience. Specifically, mysticism is here identified with contemplative prayer. This prayer is due to the action of grace upon the soul, causing the mind to know God in a different manner and the heart to love Him with an exceptional energy. Hence mysticism may be defined as *an infused loving knowledge of God*. God imparts it to the soul without the use of word, reflection or imagination. So, if it be asked how the mystical life manifests itself, the answer is: it manifests itself in prayer. If a person uses such contemplative prayer, he is in possession of

* Ibid.

the mystical life. He prays mystically and may be called a mystic even though he has never had a vision or revelation. This applies not only to persons who have enjoyed the prayer of union or ecstasy but with equal truth to those experiencing the common and almost imperceptible beginnings of mystic prayer.

Obviously we exclude contemplation as understood by St. Ignatius in the Spiritual Exercises, which apparently is a simplified type of meditation. In it the mind and imagination work in the usual way and the prayer is therefore within the scope of personal effort. Likewise we drop the distinction "acquired contemplation" – whatever it may be – and refer only to that contemplation which St. Francis de Sales, St. John of the Cross, and other masters of the spiritual life rank as the prayer immediately following upon meditation.* It is not vocal prayer, nor meditation, wherein thinking and feeling constitute the main activity. It is rather a heart-to-heart communing between the soul and its Spouse in prayer of a purely spiritual nature. Reflections and emotions are not the staple of it. The soul desires, not thoughts about God, but union with Him, and maintains itself in peace and calm, as enjoying a loving communication with Him. It is the Holy Spirit praying in the soul, and the soul concurs in loving consent.

One whom God is drawing to this grace has the beginnings of mystic prayer, otherwise known as the prayer of simplicity, of simple regard, infused prayer, the prayer of faith, interior prayer, spiritual prayer, contemplation. These expressions refer to one and the same experience under different aspects.

Thus we identify mysticism with contemplation in which, through a fresh stirring of grace, God makes Himself possessed more directly by the soul in a kind of intuition – though generally barely perceptible – of His presence. As this manner of communing with God differs so strangely from that to which the soul has been accustomed, it may be said to be secret. This accords well with the first meaning of mystical: something

---

* See Appendix.

obscure or hidden. And it is most happily called secret since the nature of this communication, from its very spiritualness, can neither be adequately described nor even distinctly understood. There are no images or concepts properly to express it. Thus it remains secret even to the soul itself.

For a better understanding of this, nothing could be so helpful as a discussion of the powers of the soul in order to observe how they function in both knowledge and prayer.

CHAPTER V

THE SOUL AND ITS POWERS

A general definition of prayer frequently given is: the converse of the soul with God. This is a broad and fair definition. But when a basis for distinguishing the various kinds of prayer is required, it must be sought in the nature of that very converse. The communion between the intelligent creature and its Creator must be held either in accordance with the soul's natural powers (something which they can effect unaided), or after some manner operated by God Himself in the soul. In the one case the soul's own activities, supernaturalized by grace, predominate; in the other they are more passive – as attentive to the action of another. With such a distinction in mind, all prayer is reducible to one or the other of two general categories: meditation or contemplation. Meditation will embrace every manner of prayer which the soul can achieve of itself, whether vocal or mental. Prayer which requires a further action of divine grace will fall under contemplation.

The soul is a spirit and therefore simple and indivisible in itself. But it operates through certain faculties or powers some of which are higher and some lower. The higher powers are the intellect and will, which exercise the functions of knowing, determining and loving. In these two powers the soul exhibits a resemblance to angelic spirits and to God.

Man, however, as a partly material being has also lower faculties, subordinated to the higher and spiritual. These lower powers correspond more directly to his sense nature. Under the intellect is the imaginative faculty. Herein are handled the images, forms and figures which have been obtained through the sense perceptions of seeing, hearing, tasting and the like. Under the will are the faculties of the sensual appetites, together with the feelings and emotions. Now it is only by means of these sense faculties that the soul can attain to an intellectual knowledge of external things. When the eye beholds an object, an image of that object is obtained in the imagination. This in turn is worked over by the intellect, which strips it of accidentals such as color, size, shape, to arrive at its essence finally as spiritualized in an idea or concept. The intellect further uses these ideas and concepts in its reflections and so advances from knowledge to knowledge. The will, as the highest appetitive faculty, follows the intellect, adhering to what appears good, rejecting what seems bad. This is the usual process of all our knowing and willing. If the exterior senses such as sight, touch, smell, were completely cut off, the soul would be as a blank, devoid of images and ideas of external things and of all knowledge save that of its own self-consciousness. Thus all our knowledge comes ultimately through channels of sense. In a similar fashion, all our converse with others (except God, with Whom we communicate by merely thinking or willing), our reception or communication of knowledge and love, must be made by the lower sense faculties, as through speaking, looking, motioning. Beyond this mode of knowing and communicating, the soul in its present state has no power, of itself, to reach.

And this is the manner employed by the soul in all prayer before contemplation. It must speak to God in terms derived from sense perception. It must use images and concepts to arouse holy affections of love. But in contemplation God Himself intervenes to engage the soul in a spiritual converse free from sense-bound activity. He begins to silence these sense labors and gives the soul to taste of a more simple operation without the aid of image, concept or reflection. This will be a prayer of simplicity, interior, mystical, free of all discursiveness.

CHAPTER VI

SIMPLER ACTIVITY OF THE SOUL

The mystical way of approach to God, of knowing, loving, and communing with Him, is a way of Faith, a purely spiritual way. Moved by grace, the soul enters its room, the doors of sense being closed, and begins to speak with its Father in secret and in spirit. In the beautiful and profound little work by Julius Tyciak called *Life in Christ,* there is a passage notable for its understanding of the nature of such prayer. It sets forth the soul's deepening sense of the mystery of God and His omnipresent action, its deepening recognition that it is *His* existence that chiefly matters, *His* operation that is essential:

> Prayer is the awakening of our consciousness of God... In prayer the soul stands exposed before God's deep-lucent eye. Then God's glance pierces into us, that glance under which the soul is matured toward God... God Himself must lay hold of us... and man must then be silent before God. Praying, man grows dumb before the Lord. But when a man has learned this sublime silence, when he has sunk before God's gaze into pure, still adoration,... he falls on his knees before love's hidden wonders, amazed and speechless in the sight of grace.*

---

* Pp. 14-15; by permission of Sheed and Ward.

Here is portrayed that simplified activity and passivity of the faculties which is the distinguishing mark of pure spiritual prayer, or contemplation. It is silent listening, quiet adoration; Mary at the feet of Jesus in reposeful love. "Be still, and see that I am God!"* This comes to pass when Our Lord begins to "lay hold." His glance pierces the soul and the prayer-life matures –even to the silencing of the powers, which are sunk before God's gaze into pure, silent adoration. This is exactly what occurs in the beginnings of mystic prayer. The sense powers used previously become, as it were, "dumb" before the Lord.

This evokes an important question. If the senses and faculties are not used but are, so to say, stilled, how then does the soul operate and how does God communicate with it?

It has been said that the channel of our knowledge and our communication is, ordinarily, sense activity. God, however, is not constrained to limit Himself to this customary working of the faculties when He would commune with the loving soul in prayer. In contemplative prayer He deals with the soul in an entirely different manner. He grants it a loving knowledge of Himself, the effect of which is to impede the faculties in their wonted activities and draw them to a more or less direct contact involving a simpler yet deeper activity of soul.

This is the more easily understood if we distinguish between the inferior and superior realms of the rational soul. Such a distinction has always been fundamental with the mystics. St. Francis de Sales treats of it brilliantly in his great *Treatise on the Love of God:*

Beyond the reason there is a certain eminence or supreme point of the reason and spiritual faculty, which is guided not by the light of argument, but by a simple view of the understanding and a simple movement of the will, by which the spirit bends and subscribes to the truth and the will of God. In this extremity and summit of our soul there is no reasoning… nothing enters but by faith… except only the

* Ps. 45:11.

high, universal and sovereign feeling that the Divine Will ought sovereignly to be loved, approved, and embraced in all things whatsoever.*

Or, again, as a late writer pictures it:

There is a higher use of the reason – without images – and this is precisely the "infused contemplation"; it is "superconscious": that is, we generally know that something is going on, but we cannot tell anyone else, or even tell ourselves, what it is, because we only describe by images. Hence, when we reflect on it, and try to put it into words, we can only call it "nothing," or vacancy; only we know really that "nothing" means "the All."†

This converse between the soul and God does not, then, take place in the intellect as reasoning but as a simplified operation which apprehends God in a kind of intuition. It does not perceive Him as such, in His essence. Neither can it see or feel Him in any describable manner. But the soul is occupied with Him in the "night of faith" wherein, by a simple view of the understanding, it apprehends Him as unlike and above and beyond all knowledge and conceptions hitherto reached by its mere reasoning powers. It perceives not so much what He is as what He is not. There is given it a strong arid unshakable conviction that He is All, that nothing else matters, that beside Him the visible universe is as if it had no being, that He alone is to be desired and loved without limit; even though the soul sees clearly that He is – and ever remains – infinitely and eternally incomprehensible.

What holds the attention, therefore, is not any kind of image, idea or impression that has come through the senses, but a spiritual impression, intangible and immaterial, yet absorbingly real. The intellect perceives nothing clearly, yet is attentive to "something" that holds it and keeps it occupied. Neither is

* Bk. I. chap. 12.
† Chapman, *Spiritual Letters,* second ed., p. 94: quoted here and elsewhere by permission of Sheed and Ward.

anything distinctly felt – unless, on occasion, according to the good pleasure of the Master. In that case it is a further infusion, special and passing, the lowest form of which is known as the Prayer of Quiet. It is the perceptible, or felt, presence of God. At one time it takes the form of a strange stillness and interior calm, a delicious recollection tending gently at times to impede bodily activity. Or again it may affect the will and emotions in a kind of commingled sweetness of soul and body. But these and such-like manifestations are distinct touches from the hand of the Beloved, which are not treated here. This work confines itself to the ordinary and more common form of mystic prayer, which is not transient but comes to endure permanently as a habit.

If, then, the mind is preoccupied with a spiritual impression, vague and indefinable, the will must accordingly be influenced by that same vague and indefinable idea, for it is the nature of the will to follow the intellect and be moved by what is set before it. Let us consult here the words of a spiritual writer, Father Grou, as set down in his well-known *Manual for Interior Souls*:

> The soul is occupied in prayer, nevertheless she does not feel that she is occupied with anything. She feels and enjoys without being able to say what she enjoys. It is no longer a particular feeling; it is a confused and general feeling which she cannot explain – always in peace, dry, distracting or consoling, but united to God in the depths of her being.

It is admittedly difficult to convey clearly what takes place in this prayer because of the absence of the particular and the distinct, but those who experience it will very likely grasp what is intimated in the description. God's infusion is an indistinct general one, which yet moves the will powerfully to love Him. This prayer may be said to be rooted in the will, for love is the most evident characteristic of it. It desires God steadily: not so much to understand, as to love, embrace, possess Him. When the soul communes with God, not by the mind thinking and reflecting, but by the deeper activity already described as concentrated in a "simple view of the understanding and a simple movement of the will," we have the essential contemplative or mystical act. It is this that constitutes the mystic, and not the incidental trappings.

A concise and yet comprehensive statement of mysticism defines it as "knowing by pure ideas after an angelic manner." This expresses the psychological process of the mystical act very well. It suggests a similarity to the angelic mode of knowing. The angels, devoid of bodily sense, receive knowledge infused directly by God. He illumines their intellects without any reasoning process. Thus their knowledge is not obtained by sense operations but by the infusion of pure ideas, ideas free of all materiality. Such a way of gaining knowledge is radically possible to man since it is the way a disembodied soul – the souls of the departed – must receive knowledge. And it seems to have been the privilege of man in the state of innocence, when his nature was not yet upset and disordered by sin. The lower powers did not impede the higher, and consequently did not tend to smother that simpler activity of soul through which he could hear without hindrance the Voice of God in the mystic language of contemplation.

Such a working of the intellect is implied in the terms adopted by the mystics themselves. They employ various expressions for the seat of its operation. Some have named it the base, ground or depth of the soul, as Père Rigoleuc (quoted by the Abbé Brémond in his interesting treatise entitled *Prayer and Poetry*):

This prayer goes on in the depth of the soul where God resides as in a secret sanctuary, far from the noise and tumult of creatures.

Blessed John Ruysbroeck calls it the supreme height:

The just man lives in a state of inviolable recollection; and even as all the multiplicities of the world cannot disturb God, so it is, in due proportion, with the soul that is united to Him; but the supreme height whither disturbance cannot reach is above the powers of the soul.

Others call it the center; still others, the apex or fine point of the spirit. Thus St. Francis de Sales:

> Now it fares in like manner with the soul who is in rest and quiet before God: for she sucks in a manner insensibly the delights of His presence, without any discourse, operation or motion of any of her faculties, save only the highest part of the will, which she moves softly and almost imperceptibly.*

These divers terms are of course metaphors to convey the idea of the intellect working after the angelic manner. All this indeed sounds high and abstruse, and unavoidably so, since it is not in the nature of contemplation that it can be clearly expressed or understood. There will always remain "something" in it obscure, hidden, mystic, but most real. "It is called mystical," observes St. Francis again, "because its conversation is altogether secret, and there is nothing said in it between God and the soul save only from heart to heart, by a communication incommunicable to all but those who make it."†

But it is not for this reason to be held as some fearfully high and lofty thing altogether beyond the range of us workaday mortals. Not at all! Perplexing as any explanation may seem, the actual thing is quite simple. And quite simple too, and unextraordinary, are the many souls who have this ordinary contemplation and beginning of mystic prayer. They would probably be startled – in the beginning, at least – if they were told that they are contemplatives; while a psychological analysis of the working of their faculties would only serve to bewilder them. The utmost reach of all simplicity is the inexplicable absolute simplicity of the Divine Essence. But what endless volumes and intricate dissertations have been made of it!

The time, however, for passing from the complex to the simpler activity – from meditation to contemplation – is to be determined by three distinct signs. And these three signs must be simultaneously present before the soul can venture to drop the one for the other.

* Op. cit., Bk. VI, chap. 9.
† Ibid.

CHAPTER VII

THE THREE SIGNS

The period of transition from discursive to contemplative prayer is the most important phase of the soul's spiritual journey, and generally the most difficult: important for the advance it marks in prayer-life and the graces of interior union; difficult because of the soul's inability to appreciate its state.

This change of prayer ordinarily comes early, especially if the way is prepared by desire for God and detachment from the world. "When this is in some degree effected," says St. John of the Cross,

> God begins at once to introduce the soul into the state of contemplation, and that very quickly, especially in the case of Religious, because these, having renounced the world, quickly fashion their senses and desires according to God; they have therefore to pass at once from meditation to contemplation. This passage takes place when discursive acts and meditation fail, when sensible sweetness and first fervors cease, when the soul cannot make reflections as before, nor find any sensible comfort, but is fallen into aridity... Souls in this state are not to be forced to meditate or to apply themselves to discursive reflections laboriously effected; neither are they to strive after sweetness and fervor, for if they did so, they would thereby be hindering the principal

agent, Who is God Himself, for He is now secretly and quietly infusing wisdom into the soul, together with the loving knowledge of Himself, without many divers distinct or separated acts.*

The three signs indicative of this transition have been explained by various authors.† A brief but sufficient discussion of them is given here.

First sign: The soul is unable to meditate. It feels a repugnance in reflecting and centering the mind on anything definite. This is experienced ordinarily only at prayer. Outside of prayer the faculties retain their customary use. Of course what is meant here is not that inability to meditate which results from voluntary distraction, neglect, fault or sin. There is question here of fervent souls in search of God.

Second sign: *The soul takes no pleasure in using the imagination or fixing it on any particular thing, earthly or heavenly.* No comfort is found either in the things of God or those of nature. The soul feels a general distaste for everything. A dryness has set in, replacing the former sweetness and facility in spiritual things. And generally – in the beginning of this state – the soul is distressed, thinking it has lost its love for God. Its prayer then is one of aridity, in which the senses, imagination and emotions find no delight and cannot be exercised.

Third sign: *The soul delights to be alone, in quiet and repose, waiting lovingly upon God, without reflecting upon anything or even desiring to do so.* "This happiness which it enjoys in thus fixing all its loving attention upon God," says Saudreau,

> makes the contemplative soul seek solitude and silence; while discharging all its social duties cheerfully, it is only happy when it is set free from them and can find itself once more alone with God... [Moreover,] this last sign persists

---

* *The Living Flame*, III, 34-37; *The Ascent of Mount Carmel*, Bk. II, chapters 13 and 14.

† De Besse, *The Science of Prayer*; Saudreau, *The Degrees of the Spiritual Life*, Vol. 2; Tanquerey, *The Spiritual Life*, pp. 663-664.

even in arid quietude, when the soul experiences a perpetual need for prayer, and seeks after solitude and silence, without, however, attaining to the enjoyment of God, all overrun as it is by every kind of preoccupation and distraction. This constant desire which it experiences to give itself up to prayer, this search, this thirst for God, shows that the will remains united to Him, and that this aridity is not a consequence of any want of fervor.*

The last sign, the soul's loving attention to God, is the decisive one of the three. If the soul did not possess it, and yet were not using the faculties discursively, it would be unoccupied, idle. The beginning of this contemplation is imperceptible to the one experiencing it because it is unfelt in the senses. It leaves them dry, in a kind of "night" in which they cannot be used. The soul is scarcely conscious of this contemplation. Perceiving nothing distinctly, its faculties useless in the way of reflecting and feeling, it thinks it is without fervor, doing nothing, wasting time.

This imperceptible contemplation, together with the aridity felt in the soul, begets an inclination toward solitude and quiet without the ability to reflect on any distinct thing. If the soul should attempt to do so, the will would experience a difficulty in withdrawing the attention from that which peacefully absorbs it. The mind cannot be attentive at once to a particular thought of its own and to that other impression, spiritual, vague and general, which is now holding it in a simple regard. That it is occupied is evident from the difficulty and strong repugnance it feels in detaching the mind from this confused, loving knowledge and fixing it on some particular image, thought or idea. Nothing can now satisfy it save the peace of remaining in God's presence in a calm, loving waiting upon Him, without any particular consideration of either God or creature.

---

*   Op. cit., Vol. 2, p. 97.

"Great, therefore," says St. John of the Cross,

is the mistake of those spiritual persons who, having labored to draw near unto God by means of imagery, forms and meditations, such as become beginners – while God would attract them to the more spiritual, interior and unseen good by depriving them of the joy and sweetness of discursive meditation – do not accept the guidance, neither know how to detach themselves from these sensible methods to which they have been accustomed. They retain these methods, still seeking to advance by them and by meditation upon exterior forms, as before, thinking that it must be so always… The soul has no pleasure in the food of the senses, but requires another of greater delicacy, interior, and less cognisable by the senses, consisting not in the travail of the imagination, but in the repose of the soul, and in the quietness thereof, which is more spiritual.*

This same spiritual impression by which God is delicately absorbing the mind and inclining the will to a simple operation of love, also acts as an impediment to vocal prayer. If one begins to say some vocal prayer he will quickly find repugnance or weariness in it, slight or pronounced according to the strength of the interior prayer. He may be able with some effort to say the words as words, but if he tries to think of their meaning, or arouse devotion by them, he will not succeed. The reason is that the attention cannot be fixed on two things at one time.

It is much the same as with a person absorbed in the reading of a book. His mind is oblivious to all else. If someone nearby addresses him, he may not be consciously aware of it for some moments. He hears the sound of the voice, but the meaning of the words will be understood only when they have penetrated his consciousness, that is, when he has withdrawn his attention from what he was reading. In the case of contemplative prayer, it is the spiritual impression absorbing the mind in a loving attention that makes it impossible for the mind to think of and

* *The Ascent of Mount Carmel,* Bk. II, chap. 12.

be attentive to something else. The simpler activity of the soul's faculties checks their discursive use, and vice versa.

Of course, nothing is said here of vocal prayers of obligation, such as the Divine Office and certain prayers imposed upon members of Third Orders. These are said in conformity to the obligations assumed. But if one's new state brings a strong abstraction of mind due to the operation of interior prayer, a material recitation will generally be the only possible one. The attention cannot be centered on the meaning of the words for the heart is attentive rather to its own loving attraction.

Generally, there will not be great difficulty. There are, however, more pronounced cases, especially in the lives of saints, where the interior operation of grace is so strong as to hinder the recitation of all vocal prayer, even the Divine Office. These instances furnish sufficient reason for dispensation, which accordingly has been given.* Poulain remarks that such cases meet the objection sometimes heard: "If your prayer thus prevents your performing exercises that are of obligation, it cannot come from God, for He would be contradicting Himself." As this author further observes:

> God is no more contradicting Himself here than when He sends an illness that hinders the hearing of Sunday Mass or the keeping of the Friday abstinence. When a law of the Church is morally impossible of execution, it ceases to oblige. God would be contradicting Himself only were He still to impose the obligation while taking away the power of fulfilling it.†

But such cases are comparatively rare. Generally in the beginning of mystic prayer the difficulty of saying vocal prayers of obligation will not be sufficient to prevent at least their material recitation, with the heart lovingly attentive to God.

---

* E. g., St. Ignatius; see Poulain, *The Graces of Interior Prayer*, p. 181.
† Ibid.; quoted by permission of B. Herder.

CHAPTER VIII

SOME IMPORTANT CONSIDERATIONS

This simple prayer is a good to be wished for with all one's heart. With it come all other goods to the soul – strength, consolation, virtue, ever-increasing union with its loving Spouse. Such prayer, indeed, belongs in the line of development of the prayer-life and has ever been considered in Catholic tradition as the likely and normal outcome of a spiritual life earnestly lived.*

Some who come to this prayer may be very imperfect. They frustrate grace because of voluntary strayings, attachments, sense indulgence, worldliness. They feel miserable because they cannot meditate, and find no relish in prayerbooks or exercises of devotion that previously brought consolation; yet because of these willful imperfections, they get nothing out of that simple prayer to which God is now drawing them. They may not be aware of what the obstacles are, or even of their own unwillingness to get rid of them. They may conclude that their apparent distaste for prayer comes from causes outside themselves. But the causes are within, in their unruly senses, interior and exterior. They yield to daydreaming, vainglorious thoughts, vindictive thoughts, imaginings of pleasures of sense

---

* See Butler, *Western Mysticism*, for the development of this general idea.

and so on. Thus they hinder God's operation and lose the grace
and profit of simple prayer.

Let the soul of good will that desires to advance and to taste
of the sweet intimacy of friendship with Jesus – let that soul
pursue its prayer seriously. Then if it finds difficulties and obstacles, these may be only apparent and not real. For the soul
must pray: it is a necessity of human nature, and should therefore be easy. The difficulty comes in our not understanding the
true nature of prayer or some of its changing phases. When one
knows this and learns to correspond to the workings of grace,
one perseveres with little trouble and soon comes to relish
prayer as that which is as natural almost as breathing. And if
grace brings one to a more affective and unitive form, a contemplative form, a prayer of the heart, there is no reason to shy
away at the idea of contemplation, or at the word mysticism, as
at some unscalable peak in the Christian and spiritual life.

Abbot John Chapman, who had an exceptionally enlightened and learned mind in all matters of prayer, has written that

> most people who use contemplative prayer are unconscious
> of anything extraordinary, except (1) the curious inability
> to meditate, (2) the ease of remaining with God, (3) and
> sometimes an "experience" that God is there. But there is
> nothing that surprises or troubles the soul, it all seems quite
> commonplace and ordinary!*

The Abbot then goes on to distinguish mystical states which are
uncommon and "the other which is very common." Regarding
this latter he continues:

> But the ordinary contemplative prayer seems to get less or-
> dinary as it develops. It gradually makes all our acts cease,
> and makes the soul in prayer receptive and passive, and ab-
> sorbs the whole life outside prayer. But even then nothing
> *happens* – there is nothing to take hold of and say: "This is a

* Op. cit., p. 261.

mystical experience; this is a revelation of divine things." It is all so calm in progress that there is no landmark.*

This ordinary contemplation is radically open to all, though indeed not all attain it. Most, apparently, never advance beyond some discursive form of prayer, except perhaps occasionally and for brief moments. The possibility is there, but varying conditions of temperament, disposition, circumstance, may affect the acquisition and practice of this prayer.

It cannot be denied that those who go on definitely for a permanent change encounter a very trying ordeal. As they lose the use of their faculties from a cause unknown to them, the change is naturally painful. They are wholly unaccustomed to this *sense-less* contact with God, which confuses and troubles them. What they now need is sympathetic understanding, instruction and encouragement. As Père Poulain observes, in the work we have already quoted:

> If we have not been instructed as to the existence of this kind of prayer, we have doubts as to the goodness of such a way. We say to ourselves: "This state is too vague to deserve the name of prayer. I must therefore try to find another." Nothing hinders our seeking, but it will generally be in vain; we cannot get out of our desert.

A difficulty here is in inducing a person whom God is leading in this way, to give up his elementary notions of prayer. At least the desire to pray is present, and this of itself is prayer. Moreover, although the person may feel he does no more at times of prayer than he does the rest of the day, that too is all passed in the wish to be united to God. And yet it may seem "like an idiotic state, and feel like the completest waste of time, until it gradually becomes more vivid."†

The conduct to be observed by the soul is, that it make no effort of its own but yield to the attraction of grace, disposing itself more and more for this rest and tranquillity. It should not

* Ibid.
† Chapman, op. cit., pp. 119-120

force itself to meditate or to make deliberate acts, such as ejaculations and the saying of prayers, or the arousing of emotions
of love. If it does it will succeed only in losing its peace and
hindering the spiritual prayer God is now perfecting in it. If
acts of love, or humility, or thanksgiving, or any others tend
to come of themselves, let them come. These are not essential,
for they are not the soul's prayer but rather accompaniments
to it. The real prayer is an interior one, going on in the depth
of the soul, in a steady desire of the heart to be lovingly attentive to God. Nor should the soul here occupy itself in trying to
feel or understand the interior operation, because this cannot
be apprehended. The soul should simply remain in peace and
repose in the presence of God. The more it accustoms itself to
this quiet and rest, free from all deliberate considerations, the
more lovingly conscious it will become of God and the sooner
it will grow in that knowledge and become established in the
habit of contemplation.

Very likely it is the experience of many a confessor, director and pastor to find souls enjoying this spiritual prayer. Both
young and old are known to visit churches or chapels and
pass long periods before the tabernacle. They seem not to get
enough of God. Without book or recitation of words, without
even telling themselves distinctly that they hunger for Him as
the Being Who alone satisfies the longings of their heart, they
are drawn to a holy peace and rest before Him. Perhaps they
have never been able to make a formal meditation as prayer but
have had a predisposition to love from the very first.

Others have prayed and meditated much and now at last
rejoice spiritually in the fruit gained by fidelity and perseverance. God is bringing them to another kind of prayer the basis
of which is a desire and longing for Him. They have distilled
the sweetness from the flowers of meditation and other spiritual exercises and now enjoy the honey of their substance,
which is divine love, in a simple view of the understanding and
a simple movement of the will. It happens much in the way of
human love. When persons first meet, they are concerned to

find things to say. Conversation must be kept up to avoid feelings of constraint. With more frequent meetings the converse becomes more easy and simple; then as friendship develops the necessity for many words is on the wane, though actually, converse between them is most natural and delightful. When love arrives they are content to say little or nothing, finding satisfaction merely in each other's presence, in a silent but deeper union of hearts.

So the loving soul, at this point, finds no satisfaction in further efforts of its own seeking. "For what indeed should she seek?" asks St. Francis de Sales in the *Treatise on the Love of God*:

> She has found Him Whom she sought, and what remains now for her but to say: "I hold Him and I will not let Him go"? She has no need to trouble herself with the discourse of the understanding, for she sees her Spouse present with so sweet a view that reasonings would be to her unprofitable and superfluous. And even if she does not see Him by the understanding she cares not, being content to feel His presence by the delight and satisfaction which the will receives from it.

Some, again – many good and well-disposed persons, and very many Religious – do feel drawn to simple prayer, but do not recognize the manifestations of it when these are present. Perceiving the tendency to calm and peace in the heart and mind, yet not understanding its meaning, they return to the support of sense activity, trying first one thing and then another, and so interfering with the operations of grace. As Chapman correctly remarks:

> Many persons pass long years in this dark night, when they cannot meditate, and yet are afraid to contemplate; and the signs may be less easy to recognize. They have tried methods, they have tried reading and pondering; alas, perhaps they have almost given up mental prayer in despair. They find it hard to believe that they are in the mystical "obscure

night." They do not feel urged to frequent thought of God, nor do they dare to say that they have a disgust of creatures. On the contrary, they have found the spiritual life so dry that they have felt thrown upon creatures for consolation; they have often taken refuge in distractions which are not sinful, because recollectedness seems impossible. They have imagined themselves to be going back, because they have no devotion, no "feeling"; and perhaps they are going back, since they have not learned the right path forward.*

From this it would appear obvious that the only sensible thing to do is to "pray as one can and not try to pray as one can't."† If one can use his powers in prayer he must do so, and he has no justification for a change in prayer. That is, if at time of prayer one can fix the imagination on some particular thought or aspect of God, Our Lord, or the truths of the faith, with facility, as one speaking to God, adoring Him, thanking or petitioning Him, he should use his faculties as he is drawn to do. In this case, evidently, no interior and spiritual impression of grace is absorbing the faculties however slightly. Then, too, it may, and usually does, happen in the beginning of the transitional period that the soul will be able at times to meditate and at other times not. This period is usually very brief.

But if the soul cannot use its powers, it simply cannot. To force a continuance of the old ways of devotion and methods of prayer when these have become tasteless and almost impossible is to oppose the call of grace and bar the way to real spiritual progress. It is all a matter of following the soul's attraction. If the soul experiences a facility in being at rest before God with a desire to be united to Him, it should remain so, not making any particular acts or efforts of its own except as it may be inclined on occasions to do so by the movements of grace. And even if it feels nothing but aridity and vague distress, still it is making an act of love toward God, for the soul desires to be in

*   Op. cit., p. 287.
†   Ibid., p. 25.

His presence, adoring Him with its entire being, to be melting in love if it were possible, even to tears. Its great anxiety is to be pleasing to God and not to offend Him in the least thing; all of which is evidence of a very high and solid love, even though the soul may feel as though it were without all love whatsoever. This same disposition of the heart, in which it lies quiet and attentive before God in a simple spirit of abandonment to Him, is to be maintained even while assisting at Mass or receiving Holy Communion.

The soul should take encouragement from the satisfaction and peace it derives when it acts thus. It is true it may not be conscious of any distinct enjoyment from this repose of the senses and loving attention of the heart. Yet it will notice an unwillingness to be diverted from it. And if the soul should ask itself: What would I rather be doing than this?, it would have to answer: Nothing; or, Where would I prefer to be rather than here?, it would have to admit: Nowhere. It simply finds a quiet happiness in thus remaining in God's presence.

All this should reassure the soul and give it confidence. But such is our poor nature that it ever tends to be gravitating toward sense activity, finding not enough satisfaction in the purely spiritual. Self seeks assertion. It wants to be doing something, or feeling that it is accomplishing something or getting somewhere, and it chafes at subjugation to more spiritual operations and realities.

CHAPTER IX

POINTS OF DIFFICULTY AND ENCOURAGEMENT

Since the soul generally feels estranged as it enters upon this period, it will greatly need to be consoled and encouraged. Everything is so unaccustomed, it hardly knows what to do or where to turn. Its usual conduct in this changing state of prayer is to resist the new direction of grace or at least fail to co-operate with it properly. It may also have fears of delusion. Lacking its former feelings of devotion, it thinks itself incapable of devotion, and believes it is going backward; hence the idea of advance seems to it an error.

Besides this, it will experience a repugnance in speaking of its condition. If it attempts to set this forth, it can find nothing specific to say. When questioned as to what it does in prayer, how it spends the time, it seems embarrassed and at a loss for an answer. It stammers, searching for phrases to describe what cannot easily be put into words. It may even declare it does nothing, or at least feels that it does nothing, which lends color to the fear of delusion.

The only definite thing to be got from these souls is that they are generally contented and satisfied – though not knowing really why – and so feel disinclined to follow a suggestion or line of conduct that will interfere with their loving attention to God and tie them down to some particular act or thing. A soul in this state says of itself: "I always give in to this attraction, and although I cannot perceive that it guides me well, I cannot help following it. I have an assurance, I do not know how, in the depths of my heart, that this way is right; not by the evidence of my senses but by a feeling inspired by faith."* Moreover, it may truly be said that "its whole state and way is simply an impression of the gift of faith, which makes it love and appreciate those paths wherein the spirit has neither object nor idea," and wherein "the bride recognizes the Bridegroom unconsciously. She prefers to wander without order or method in abandoning herself to His guidance than to gain confidence by following the beaten tracks of virtue."†

But despite this sure guidance of faith, nature is ever clamoring to be heard. It wants to have that feeling of support, whether in emotions of fervor or through the satisfaction of some self-activity. As De Caussade so well writes to one in this condition:

> What you want is to find support and comfort in yourself and your good works. Well, this is precisely what God does not wish, and what He cannot endure in souls aspiring after perfection. What! lean on yourself! count on your works! Could self-love leave a more miserable fruit? God desires to deliver you from all this and to destroy in you gradually all the help and confidence you derive from yourself so that He may be your sole support and hope.‡

What augments the distress and discouragement in the beginning is the matter of distractions. The imagination frequently seems overrun with thoughts and images. When prayer is of a more consoling nature, carrying some sweetness in it, the soul is less troubled about distractions, but as it becomes a prayer of aridity the distractions seem naturally more pronounced.

---

* De Caussade, *Abandonment to Divine Providence*, p. 74.
† Ibid., p. 75.
‡ Ibid., p. 341.

But here again the distinction between the superior and inferior portions of the soul is to be borne in mind. If the distractions are voluntary and occupy the attention of the intellect, they obviously stop spiritual prayer, and have to be actively opposed. But if they are images that come and go merely in the imagination so that the attention of mind and heart is not centered on them, they do not impede the act of simple prayer. This prayer goes on in the superior part of the rational soul, above reasoning and reflection, beyond images and ideas, and so cannot be hindered by what goes on in the lower faculty, in the imagination. So long as the will or heart is toward God and wants only Him, the soul need not be troubled from the fact of distractions. Far different is it with a person using discursive prayer, which employs images, ideas, affections and reflections; any distraction here would necessarily take the soul out of prayer and away from God. In ordinary mystic prayer, neither thinking, feeling nor imagining plays any part, but the mind and heart are occupied in a confused, general, loving knowledge of God in the center of the soul.

Undoubtedly the soul will find it irksome at times to be still before God, to remain in His presence in the simple spirit of faith. Yet this is the way it must now co-operate with the workings of grace, for the Holy Spirit is gently drawing it to the interior. He is espousing the soul to Him in faith.

The soul may wonder how long a condition so distasteful to the senses will last. With it all there may be the feeling of being abandoned by God, because the soul has lost all feelings of devotion. Sometimes it is not certain whether it loves God or not, or whether God loves it. This is very painful, but purifying. The soul must be encouraged to remain in the peace and tranquillity wherein God is truly found, and not to stir up natural activity in the way of reflections or ejaculations, which is only a return to sense operations. Its spirituality is now founded upon the strength of faith and not upon the weakness of sense. Consequently it must not attempt to force fervor or the feelings of it, or take up any kind of particular devotion with a view to gaining satisfaction or assurance that something is thereby accomplished. Such a course would only beget a multiplicity contrary to that simplicity of spirit to which God is drawing it. And the more simple it is interiorly, the better prepared it is for divine union. So the soul has merely to yield to the attraction it feels for quiet repose, to be susceptible and docile to the communications and inspirations of grace.

The essence of this common form of mystic prayer is the desire for God. The soul feels only this one desire and need, and its time is generally spent in groping after God – though it may be unconsciously. This desire for God is of course a spiritual activity of the will and is not manifested in feelings of affection or emotions of fervor; hence it is trying to mere nature. But the soul will gradually learn that not what can be "felt" matters, but what is above feeling; that not what can be "seen" is of value, but what is beyond sight. Flesh and sense are insipid to the spirit – not having the victorious power of that faith which is now the source of the soul's growing strength and contact with God, and which makes it persevere "as if seeing Him Who cannot be seen."*

This obscure way of faith, which is the truly mystic and contemplative way, may in its more arid and hidden manifestation last for years. To whatever degree of strength it develops, even the most extraordinary, the element of obscurity remains, because it is a way of faith and not of sense. This is evident in the lives of the saints. When St. Jane de Chantal was questioned about her prayer she replied that it was a time of helplessness, of almost stupidity; she hardly knew how to describe it. She remained in this state for many years. Yet it was this very mystic and arid prayer that wrought her sanctification, and to which she was ever inclined. She writes:

> His Goodness bestowed upon me this method of devotion consisting in a simple beholding and realizing of His Divine Presence, in which I felt at rest with Him… By my

* Heb. 11:27.

unfaithfulnesses I have opposed it much; permitting entrance into my mind of fears of being useless in this condition, so that, desiring to do somewhat on my part, I spoiled all. And yet ofttimes am I attacked by this very fear, not in this devotion but in my other exercises, where I would ever be active and multiplying acts, although well aware that I thus drew myself from my center; above all, I see that this unique and simple looking toward God is my only remedy and sole consolation. And, certainly, did I follow my inclination, I should do nought but this without exception. For when I think to fortify my soul with thoughts and discourses, resignations and acts, I expose myself to new temptations and difficulties, and can only do it by a violent effort which leaves me dry. So it behooves me to return promptly to this simple abandonment.*

Here is an exceptionally clear expression of this state of spiritual prayer. The saint dwells on the tendency of mere nature to oppose the sweet attractions of divine grace and to be ever harping on its own activities, though without success. It is hard to kick against the goad. Yet her deepest inclination was to remain at her center in a peaceful, simple looking toward God. At times the prayer may indeed become more vivid by a further development or impulse of grace. But the ordinary state is that which she has depicted, and concerning which she writes in another place:

There are certain souls among those whom God leads by this way of simplicity, whom He strips of all satisfaction, desire and feeling so that they can scarce endure or express themselves, because what is passing within them is so slight, delicate and imperceptible, being wholly centered in the extreme point of the spirit, that they cannot speak of it.†

---

* Quoted by Brémond in *A Literary History of Religious Thought in France*, Vol. II, p. 406; by permission of the Macmillan Company.
† Ibid.

The soul finds in this condition, with the attendant difficulties, a fruitful source of worry and anxiety. And when it consults its confessor or director, it can at most only get assurance that it is going right, and a little encouragement to persevere. As to the director himself, he is confidently reassured by these and similar reactions. The frequent self-examinations of the penitent, together with the vague and confused nature of his questions, offer a clue to go by. Sometimes the signs may not be so clear, yet the essential characteristics are there. Saudreau lists a number of test points indicative of the contemplative way. He asks, for instance:

1. Is the soul repelled by considerations and by discursive prayer?

2. Does it perform duties more from duty than inclination, seeking consolation in prayer only?

3. Does it experience a vague, unreasoned but profound distaste for everything that is not God, or does not bear relation to Him?

4. Does it feel a quiet happiness in being alone with God – without having anything special to say to Him?*

In such a state one need not fear delusion, attributing it to imagination or pretence. This prayer cannot be simulated, and it rather comes as a surprise to one to find he is in the mystic state. It is all so different from what he might have expected, imagined or read about, and so uncongenial to nature. It may even seem to be nothing at all, a waste of time, for there is not anything there for the imagination or senses to lay hold of. It is truly the way of blind faith, yet from it the soul does get a certain satisfaction of peace, barely felt, because spiritual and in the depth of the soul.

Another peculiarity of this state is the soul's choice of spiritual reading. Previous to the appearance of interior prayer, only

---

* *The Degrees of the Spiritual Life*, Vol. II.

such books as dwelt on the particular and the definite brought satisfaction and profit, such as ascetical works, treatises on the virtues, or the lives of certain saints. But mystical prayer brings a taste and desire for mystical writings, for books dealing with contemplation. The soul finds in such reading "something" that corresponds in some manner to its present state, an echo of its own experience. A person not walking in this path will get less, or perhaps nothing at all, in the way of help or satisfaction from reading of this kind. His will is moved only by the distinct, the clear, the definite, and these are necessary to occupy his faculties. But those in the way of mystic prayer are moved only by the indistinct, the obscure, the general – in a word, by that impression of faith, spiritual and intangible, through which they enjoy a loving knowledge of God.

The sum and substance of it is that the soul should at all costs persevere in prayer, resolved not to relax, or be overcome by discouragement, or give up for any reason whatsoever. Whether in dejection or elation, let it firmly and confidently pursue its daily practice. Let it have courage and trust worthy of the loving God Who is leading it safely and happily on the path He intends. With this prayer comes all the soul's good, its holiness, its happiness. And even though at times the prayer is distressing or distracting, miserable or dull, invaded by worry and anxiety, let the soul remember the advice of the Abbot Chapman:

> Possibly the best kind of prayer is when we are unable to do anything, if then we throw ourselves on God, and stay contentedly before Him; worried, anxious, tired, listless, but – above all and under it all – humbled and abandoned to His will, contented with our own discontent. If we can get ourselves accustomed to this attitude of soul, which is always possible, we have learned how to pray, and we can pray for any length of time – the longer the better –and at any time.*

---

*   Op. cit, p. 133.

Thus it is evident that prayer is the more excellent the less sensible it is and the less perceptible to the soul. It would be a mistake, then, to think one is not praying unless he uses discursive prayer; to think nothing is accomplished except by speaking, thinking, feeling. And great would be the mistake, too, in seeking to remain in these elementary forms when grace speaks by way of the mystic, spiritual, interior prayer of the heart.

CHAPTER X

A FEAR REMOVED

The apparent inactivity and repose of the faculties in contemplative and mystic prayer will at once raise a question in some minds as to the deception of quietism. The writer can recall the cautious fears of a person whom God was long calling to the repose of contemplation. "But isn't there a danger? How can I be certain I am not falling into quietism?" When the question was put point-blank, "What is quietism?," the person answered in humble confusion, "I do not know."

One might, of course, confuse the quiet of the faculties in contemplation with the error of quietism: the very expressions employed offer basis for the confusion. But nothing could be further from the truth. Because the powers are in repose, it is not to be concluded that the soul is inactive. On the contrary, the soul is active, with a simplified activity coming from the inmost being, in which the will from its depths adheres to God. It is like an act of faith, made in the higher part of the soul and imperceptible to the senses. This simple movement of the will in adhering to God is the very highest activity. Contemplation is at once repose and intense action. In this it faintly resembles a characteristic of the Divine Being, Who though He is Pure Activity remains forever undisturbed in unchangeable repose.

In his study, *The Graces of Interior Prayer*, Père Poulain writes:

Quietists teach all action is an imperfection, and that the immobility of our faculties must therefore be an "ideal" toward which all our endeavors should tend. Hence the name quietists.... But because the prayer of simplicity has been thus extolled by the quietists, we need not conclude that it is dangerous, for we should then fall blindly into a snare set for us by the devil. When he cannot make a direct attack upon practices that are inspired by God, he tries to bring them into discredit by exaggerations or an admixture of falsehood. These practices thus become suspected even by well-intentioned persons who have not the leisure or the talent to separate the good grain from the tares.*

There are many angles to the quietistic error all of which may be reduced to this root tenet: the Divine Being can be experimentally found or perceived in our consciousness if only we remove all obstacles.† The word to be noted here is experimentally. A definition often given of mystical prayer is that it is an experimental knowledge of God, a kind of perception of God in the soul. Doubtless He is ever truly present to the soul in grace, but a conscious perception and enjoyment of Him cannot be had by the soul's unaided powers. This requires the added touch of the Finger of God when and as He pleases. To force an artificial and self-imposed quiet upon mind and imagination – no action of divine grace intervening – leaves the soul wholly inactive. It does nothing itself, and it receives nothing from God. It is His action that must draw the soul to repose and move it to act in a higher way.

There is a break between meditation and contemplation, the latter being the result of a new action of grace. And though the beginnings of mystic prayer may not be easily perceptible, the direct part played by God in it should be recognizable by all.

The quietist, however, denies this very thing – at least implicitly. If we can experience contact with Divinity simply by removing all obstacles, mystical prayer will be considered exclusively as the achievement of our own personal effort. For

---

* Pp. 59-60.

† See Howley, *Psychology and Mystical Experience*, chapter on "Quietism."

this reason quietist writers placed such strong emphasis on the negative side of asceticism, the utmost stripping of self-activity. This was extended particularly to the activities of mind and will. Not only all thoughts, imaginations and reflections were to be cast out but the will itself must cease to desire. This was carried to such an absurd extreme as to include the desire for sanctity and even salvation; one must not even strive for virtue or resist temptation. The error in this is evident. In genuine contemplative prayer, it is true, the action of God gradually absorbs that of the soul, but the will must ever exercise its own activity in co-operating, giving unceasing consent to God's action. Some quietists rejected even this consent as being activity and therefore worthless.

All writers, both orthodox and quietist, insist on the clearing away of the obstacles to divine union. A main purpose of ascetic practice is to subject the appetites and passions to the control of reason. Included in this is the aim of curtailing sense activity with a view to establishing the soul in peace for its meeting with God in prayer. Such is surely the most fitting preparation for spiritual contact with the purity and simplicity of the Divine Being. It is a training in evangelical perfection. But further than this the soul cannot go of itself; it must await the action of grace as this reveals itself in a new manner.

Here is the saving reason for the three signs. What preserves one from quietism is precisely their simultaneous presence. They indicate the divine action; and if the soul had not this justification, its faculties would indeed be idle, empty, quietistic. But the quietist ignores any signs. He goes by his own action, which procedure is a brand of self-hypnosis. In true contemplation it is the action of grace which draws the soul to loving repose in God.

There is another point of reassurance on the practical side. The test of prayer is its effect on daily life. Advance in virtue, horror of sin, remorse at willful faults, imply a good prayer. The will derives power from it and a false prayer could not produce such results. The quietist, on the other hand, is likely to fall away from virtuous living. He gets nothing from God. His strength is from himself – which accounts for the notable aberrations and moral lapses in the lives of some outstanding advocates of quietism. But here, as always, false doctrine is best dispelled by exposition of the true.

CHAPTER XI

TWO VIRTUES

In view of the preceding, it is well to say a few words on those virtues that are unquestionably most essential for souls advancing on the path of interior union with God. The two to be stressed are humility and obedience. On these rests the very foundation of all spiritual life. Without them our supernatural life would have neither truth nor security, and we should soon lose our way in a wilderness of pride and self-love.

Now it is an evident fact, clearly reflected in the lives of all holy and Christlike persons, that the necessary predisposition for the reception of God's gifts and graces is humility of heart. "He that is a little one, let him come to Me."... "Where humility is, there also is wisdom."* And it may be truly said that where God does not find at least the beginnings of this fundamental virtue, or the effort to attain it, He will refrain from communicating those gifts with which He so ardently longs to adorn the human soul. Indeed, it is a kind of law in the kingdom of God that all ascent and approach to His throne is by way of the ladder of humility; and the greater the saint in the kingdom, the more deeply penetrated is his soul with this lovely virtue. It is humility that not only attracts the hearts of men but endears

* Prov. 9:4; 11:2.

the soul to God, arresting His loving glance so that He beholds it with divine complacency.

"Behold the handmaid of the Lord,"* said the humblest and meekest of all God's creatures: she who is the most richly endowed, the Jewel of all creation. And even the Sacred Humanity of Jesus paid the price – as a condition, so to speak – of its unique gift of hypostatic union with the second Person of the Godhead by an unparalleled humility and humiliation. Wherefore St. Paul could wish nothing better for the Christian and child of God:

> Have this mind in you which was also in Christ Jesus, Who though He was by nature God, did not consider being equal to God a thing to be clung to, but emptied Himself, taking the nature of a slave and being made like unto men. And appearing in the form of man, He humbled Himself, becoming obedient to death, even to death on a cross. Therefore God has exalted Him and has bestowed upon Him the name that is above every name, so that in the name of Jesus every knee should bend of those in heaven, on earth and under the earth, and every tongue should confess that the Lord Jesus Christ is in the glory of God the Father.†

The further advanced we are in the supernatural life and the nearer we are to God, the humbler in all truth we must be. Every devout person, then, will naturally beg for this most engaging virtue of humility. Such a course will save many a one from going astray; for, in contrast to the darkness that inevitably follows in the wake of pride, the wisdom that comes with humility enlightens the soul. And if we do perceive some gift or grace in ourselves – as the saints could not help but observe in themselves – we, like them, will disclaim anything as our own, except sin and misery, but will lay the gift to the sheer mercy of Infinite Goodness.

---

* Luke 1:38.
† Phil. 2:6-11.

Where the prayer is true and persevering, moreover, humility will appear as a fruit. It is, indeed, an unfailing work of spiritual prayer, to beget this virtue in proportion to its own advance; the deeper the prayer-union, the deeper the humility. The sense of helplessness in the powers of the soul, a feeling even that its spirituality is gone, as well as a perception of its shortcomings due to closer contact with God, tend to keep it humble. Finding little of the satisfaction it once did in many spiritual activities, the soul is more likely to be cast down at sight of its own poverty, and to consider others better than itself. This causes the soul to lose, too, its former deep attachment to its own ideas of spirituality and goodness, and instead to feel embarrassed at a word of praise. Besides, any falls and imperfections that may occur at this stage will further maintain it in loving humility.

The twin virtue to humility is obedience. It may even be considered as a phase or offshoot of humility insofar as obedience is humility of mind, submission of will and judgment to another. It is precisely this submission to ecclesiastical and spiritual authority that preserves the Christian from error. Many have fallen, as in the case of the quietists, who perhaps had notable qualities and distinctions; but they lacked obedience to lawful authority. Wherever this occurs, wherever there is contempt and disdain for the guidance that God has willed to set up in this world, there too is illusion, loss of the way and, not infrequently, permanent disaster.

Such deceptions have often been known in the matter of private inspirations, visitations, communications and revelations. All genuinely holy souls will – as the saints have done – in every instance refer whatever personal communications and spiritual experiences they may receive, whatever be the message, to the proper guide and authority in God's Holy Church. Any deviation on this point is sure sooner or later to lead to error, if not in doctrine at least in practice.

Suppose, then, some inspiration comes by way of prayer. This is the moment to remember that the ecclesiastical or religious

Superior is the representative of God for those under his or her care; therefore, obedience to the Superior is obedience to God. But what if God demands one thing in prayer and the Superior, incredulous, demands the opposite? No doubt God, knowing our reluctance to obey, may on occasion prompt something which He knows the Superiors will not permit. In this case, what He really wants is the sacrifice of one's will, which is the supreme act of personal adoration that can be offered to Him. Therefore – always presupposing there is no question of sin – we must undoubtedly obey our Superiors. We are never so sure of inspirations we think divine as of the commands of lawful authority, wherein the will of God is plainly signified to us.

Such was the instruction of Our Lord to St. Margaret Mary. He told her on one occasion that He would adjust His graces to the spirit of the rule, to the will of her Superiors, and that she must regard with suspicion anything that would withdraw her from exact obedience. And He further bade her to prefer her Superiors' orders to His, saying (as we read in Bougaud's life of this saint) that He would know how to accomplish His designs in His own way.

"He who hears you, hears Me,"* He said to those who bear His authority. And the truly humble and spiritual soul will abase itself under all rather than trust to its own unenlightened guidance. Even St. John of the Cross, outstanding teacher in spiritual and contemplative matters though he was, humbly wrote in the Prologue to his work:

> I accept the aid of experience and learning, and if through ignorance I should err, it is not my intention to depart from the sound doctrine of our Holy Mother the Catholic Church. I resign myself absolutely to her light, and submit to her decisions, and moreover to the better judgment herein of private men, be they who they may.†

---

* Luke 10:16.
† Prologue to the *Ascent*.

The soul, then, can make no mistake in obedience. On occasion it may receive unsuitable advice; but where no sin is involved, it acts rightly in obeying. It is a very easy thing for God to bring the soul in the providential path of one who will give the needed counsel; and He does this frequently. Meanwhile, victory is granted to the humble and obedient heart.

CHAPTER XII

ACCOMPANYING EFFECTS OF THIS PRAYER

As contemplative prayer brings about such a marked change in the manner of the soul's interior operation, it is natural that there should be a corresponding modification all along the line of the spiritual course. The entire life is affected. The inner result is a wonderful simplifying and unifying of the soul's activities. Our merely natural bent is toward multiplicity, whether in temporal or in spiritual things. This is now checked under the influence of simple prayer, which attracts the soul more and more to simplicity in everything. The action of the Holy Spirit ever tends to draw the soul away from multiplicity, whether inwardly – to lead it gently to the unity that is Himself – or outwardly – to seek the "one thing needful."*

The great desire of the soul is to be ever finding its Lord in the loving repose of prayer. Contemplation has become its main exercise, the central longing of its heart. To this all other occupations are subordinated. Duties are now done not so much out of the natural enthusiasm that springs from self as out of the supernatural love engendered in simple prayer. God has come to fill the consciousness of the soul, to be its very All. In the beginning this effect is so pronounced that the soul longs to be alone, away in solitude, desiring neither to hear, know, or speak of anything of this world. These matters have become strange to it. Hence we find written in the Spiritual Journal of

---

* Luke 10:42.

Lucie Christine, the revealing account which Father Poulain
has edited:

> What makes the soul really suffer is when one is obliged to
> lend one's attention to some banal, worldly conversation.
> The soul then feels ill at ease, estranged by all the insignifi-
> cant things she hears, and to which she must make some re-
> ply. She compares these empty words to the Divine Silence
> of the Church and of the Tabernacle, and the heart is home-
> sick for the altar.

God's own working in the soul has estranged it from sensible and temporal things to give it a taste for the Divine. The
only satisfying diet is the general, obscure, loving knowledge
of Himself that God is infusing into it. It relishes only peace,
quiet, and whatever tends to the calm of recollection. After
some period, shorter or longer – in certain cases extending
over several years – when it has become accustomed to its new
prayer, it once again adjusts itself to the particular; yet it remains detached, for it sees and handles all under the light of a
deeper faith. And precisely because the soul is detached from
all things and attached only to God and His Holy Will, it can
find a higher kind of use and appreciation of created things.
They do not now absorb the soul and entangle it in affections
and allurements that tend to upset the passions and promote
sense activities.

There is also some outward manifestation of this inward
simplicity and unity of spirit. It affects not only the bearing and
conduct generally but even the matter of devotions. Since to be
at peace before God is the soul's one desire, its former multi-
farious practices will be reduced to simplification. The Master
Himself is leading it to the more continuous operation of love
wherein all else is absorbed. Thus if it has hitherto practiced
what is known as the particular examen, it now finds a difficulty in doing so. The same repugnance it experiences in exciting
its faculties to meditate is felt in examining the conscience and
analyzing its motives and actions. However, this is more than

compensated for by the mystic prayer which throws immediate light on the soul's conduct, and causes it distinct pain the moment it commits a voluntary fault. As it lives now constantly in the Will of God, whatever is contrary to that Holy Will becomes grievous to it. And this growing union with its Spouse which persists throughout the day renders it ever watchful lest it offend Him in anything, however small. Here again, what could scarcely be achieved by one's own effort, readings and reflections, is now wrought almost without labor by the power emanating from interior prayer.

Again, this simplification applies even in the matter of explicit intentions made in prayer. Some souls are reduced to such a loving simplicity in things spiritual as to dwell, so to say, in the very atmosphere of love. It is difficult for them to form particular intentions. Their distaste for doing so may at first distress them, until they arrive at a truer understanding of prayer. The case comes to mind of a person who was long led to contemplation without suspecting it. This person was working against the call of grace for several years by forcing endless particular acts and devotions, not only in an effort to enkindle some feeling of fervor but especially with a view to liberating the soul of a deceased relative. This apparently was the substance of the prayer-life, and it was hindering progress if not causing a distaste for prayer. When this person was instructed how to correspond with the action of the Holy Spirit, everything became clear and a new and simplified spiritual life began.

Such persons may think they are not helping departed relatives and friends without making explicit applications and intentions, but they must come to understand that their new way of prayer is the way of unceasing love, and is so vastly pleasing to the Heavenly Spouse, the infinitely generous Divine Lover, that He will grant all and more than they could obtain in particular intentions. For this God of all consolation, Who searches the reins and the heart, is delighted to anticipate the intentions and requests of the loving soul. So we are not to force ourselves but must ever yield to the sweet operations of love, not making any more interior acts than we feel impelled to under the impulse of the Spirit of God.

The state of a soul so well established in contemplation that this is used habitually in prayer, is excellently described by Father Grou, one of the finest spiritual writers of the eighteenth century:

> Everything, therefore, that God does to a soul to make it holy, has for its first object to make it simple; and all the co-operation He requires from that soul is that it should allow itself to be torn from every kind of multiplicity, to pass on to a state of simplicity… When, therefore, a soul has given herself entirely to God,… He simplifies her first of all in the very depths of her nature by placing there a principle of infused and supernatural love which becomes the simple and only motive of her whole conduct… She refers everything to this love, without even thinking expressly about it… God makes her simple in her understanding. The multitude of thoughts that formerly embarrassed her, ceases; during this time she can no longer meditate, or reason or speak. A light that is simple, though indistinct, enlightens her.… This soul is always the same, even when she is not actually in prayer; if she is reading, or speaking, or occupied with work and domestic cares, she feels that she is less taken up with what she is doing than with God… and that He is really the secret occupation of her spirit… She goes simply as God leads her.*

If previously the soul desired to do this or do that, to seek this diversion or that relaxation or amusement, it does so no longer. If once it took the initiative in the interests and expressions of self, it now corresponds to the initiative of grace. And in doing so it finds peace, the peace that lies in the will of Him "Who moves the sun in heaven and all the stars."†

---

* *Manual for Interior Souls*, pp. 386-387.
† Dante, end of *Paradiso*.

These accompanying effects and characteristics of common mystic prayer are experienced generally, and in varying degrees. Much depends on the depth and progress of the prayer. But in any case, it gives proof of a powerful interior principle at work in the soul, which indeed becomes the soul's greatest treasure, giving it a distinct satisfaction in being able to live and be guided at this fine point of the spirit.

It is evident that ordinary mystic prayer, whether dry or consoling, has unusual efficacy. As it comes to be the soul's habitual prayer, it is natural that it should reflect itself in divers effects. In fact, this obscure prayer is felt more in its effects than in itself. It ever works toward transforming the soul into Christ, endowing it with the heart and mind of Him Who is the Source and the Exemplar of all true holiness. The mind, enlightened by a simple spiritual wisdom, judges things supernaturally and in the light of Eternal Truth with a penetration not possessed by carnal wisdom.

> The sensual man does not perceive the things that are of the Spirit of God, for it is foolishness to him and he cannot understand, because it is examined spiritually. But the spiritual man judges all things, and he himself is judged by no man. For "who has known the mind of the Lord, that he might instruct Him?" But we have the mind of Christ.*

In the light of this wisdom many faults and imperfections hitherto hidden are revealed to the soul. This inclines it to humility inasmuch as its true self is being unmasked, and it sees that it has nothing, is nothing, and can do nothing, of itself. Besides, repeated falls have shown it its own helplessness, and made it know the words of its Saviour: "Without Me you can do nothing."† God's greatness, on the other hand, stands out clearer than ever. The soul sees that He is the Lord and Father of all; that nothing can endure without Him; that it is He Who "spreadeth out [the heavens] as a tent to dwell in," and "hath

* I Cor. 2:14-16.
† John 15:5.

poised with three fingers the bulk of the earth";* that He alone can "join together the shining stars, the Pleiades," or "put wisdom in the heart of man";† and it wants to spend its being in singing the glories of this great God.

Even more noticeable than the spiritual illumination of the mind is the touch of energy communicated to the will. Formerly the soul made resolutions again and again and failed in their fulfillment. Now it may seldom make a resolution yet it steadily and easily observes the former ones. The senses have been weakened and the higher faculties strengthened so that acts of virtue or self-denial are practiced with little effort. Moreover, the soul has now the general resolution of denying itself and serving God in everything. And this renunciation is not some manner of ascetic gymnastics, wherein may exist a preoccupation merely with the ways and means of perfection. Rather the moving spirit is love, a love concerned not so much with a self-sought perfection as with a Being – to Whom it feels the need of surrendering itself utterly.

Thus, a great generosity is born of this spiritual prayer. The soul yields itself to God, realizing at last the implication of the Great Commandment: "Thou shalt love the Lord thy God with thy whole heart, and with thy whole soul, and with thy whole strength, and with thy whole mind."† The wisdom God grants it forces it sweetly to seek its occupation, recreation and happiness in Him alone; it is consequently unable to derive comfort and satisfaction elsewhere. Thus it lives by the single eye of faith, which makes the whole body lightsome to run in the way of the Lord. And since God is now refreshing the soul spiritually, it is fitting that it should lose the taste for other things, that it may sing with St. John of the Cross:

> He that is on fire with love
> Divinely touched of God,

---

*   Isa. 40:22, 12.
†   Job 38:31, 36.
†   Luke 10:27.

Receives a taste so new
That all his own is gone.
Like one who of a fever ill
Loathes the food before him,
And longs for what I know not,
Which happily is found.*

Here is the reason for its loathing food of earthly desire – the fire of divine love, enkindling in the soul a longing for "it knows not what." It knows no name for it because it is an impression of faith without form or figure; not within the scope of mere sense knowledge. Yet in this intangible, indefinable "something" that secretly engages it, the soul recognizes its Divine Lover, Whom it has truly found, and Who nourishes in it the attraction of ever finding Him in the peaceful repose of interior prayer.

A settled peace – felt or unfelt – has come to it. The senses are mortified, the passions set in order. And as it perseveres and advances in its new way, it finds within itself a living hope in God which, says St. John of the Cross,

> fills the soul with such energy and resolution, with such aspiration after the things of eternal life, that all this world seems to it – as indeed it is – in comparison with what it hopes for, dry, withered, dead and worthless. The soul now denudes itself of the garments and trappings of this world, by setting the heart upon nothing that is in it, and hoping for nothing that is, or may be, in it, living only in the hope of everlasting life. And when the heart is thus lifted up above the world, the world cannot touch it or lay hold of it, nor even see it.†

When the soul sees itself in this happy disposition, living with a joy grounded upon nothing of this world but upon the hope of everlasting life, let it rejoice and be glad. And if it longs for heaven with at times a holy impatience, let it do so

---

* *Poems:* "God the Supreme Good," stanza 3.
† *The Dark Night of the Soul,* Bk. II, chap. 21.

unabashed – yet abandoned to God – for it has found the pearl of great price.

These are some of the effects wrought by interior prayer, and the consideration of them should help the soul over the difficulties, trials, desolations, feelings of insensibility and the like which accompany this prayer. What could be a surer sign of the soul's spiritual health than a longing for God, an inability to find comfort outside Him, a steady fear of displeasing Him, an attraction to prayerful solitude? Such a state is one of great grace and blessing, for which the soul, whether in sweetness or in desolation, sings its gratitude in the secret language of mystic prayer.

CHAPTER XIII

ASCETICISM AND MYSTICISM

Mystical prayer is free of formal method. Its very spirituality precludes such method as might be used, for instance, in meditation. There will accordingly be no "schools"
of mysticism. Its one and only school is that of the Holy Spirit,
Who teaches and draws the soul from within. Different souls
traverse different paths to mystic prayer, but that prayer essentially follows one law – the law of wordless, imageless, heart-
to-heart contact with God. God may grant special infusions of
grace and divine touches which enkindle flames of love, but
that which constitutes the mystic way is the indefinable communication experienced in the depths of the soul by a simple
view of the understanding and a simple movement of the will.
And since this is chiefly God's work, there can hardly be human
schools of mystic practice.

But there are schools of asceticism, for asceticism is the human preparation and cultivation of the ground in which the
seed of grace is to fructify. Asceticism has not to do with prayer
as such, but with ways of spiritual training. The ascetic side is,
therefore, the side of the soul's natural activity, and proposes
for practice whatever is necessary to build up the structure of
Christian perfection. The schools of asceticism are distinguish-
able by the emphasis placed on particular doctrines and ways of
life, or by the distinctive spirit imparted by the various religious
founders. Each order or congregation inherits a characteristic

spirit and work to do. Each has its own method of training in perfection – though all aim at fostering divine union, including preparation for mystic union.

However, the mystical life is not a continuation of the ascetical life in the sense that when the former is found the latter ceases. On the contrary, ascetic practice goes on step by step with mystic prayer. But with the appearance of the latter, the ascetic phase assumes a more passive character. The soul denies itself, certainly, but not with such positive joy in the performance of particular acts. Rather it experiences a general act of renunciation, a habitual disposition of universal detachment in which the demands of the inferior nature lose their strength. Besides, the soul now sees the superiority of God's work over its own, the disposition of His Providence in which the soul suffers abandonment, or darkness, various moral and spiritual sufferings. It is further mortified by its own interior humiliations, its consciousness of its many hidden faults and failures in practicing virtue and in reacting to the sudden and unexpected trials that come from the circumstances of daily life.

All this is felt by the soul to work a more purifying effect than its own feeble efforts. Self-activity becomes co-operation, in which the soul yields itself more to the action of Another – Who moves the will sweetly in all things, giving it strength and facility in the way of the Cross. The soul no longer seems to wish for anything in particular, but rather, in simplicity of spirit, refers all to the love of God. This apparently is the "most noticeable characteristic of the spiritual life of contemplatives: instead of loving God for intelligible reasons, instead of serving Him throughout the day for definite motives, they feel they are carried along by grace."* And very quickly their main practice comes to be a simple abandonment to the Divine Will in everything.

But even though the action of God gains the ascendancy, a careful self-denial and watch over the senses must be

* Chapman, op. cit., p. 318, footnote.

maintained lest the desires of sense come quickly to the fore again. Immortification, pandering to sense, dissipation of spirit, cultivation of attachments, self-will, worldliness – each and all of these stifle the language of mystic prayer, silencing the Divine Voice in the depths of the soul. Any willful, unrejected attachment to an imperfection will be contrary to that pureness and liberty of spirit requisite for enjoying the calm, loving knowledge of God. When the human will is disattuned, however slightly, to the divine, it cannot rest in that peaceful, loving attention to God which is the characteristic activity of ordinary mystic prayer.

In this passive way all comes eventually to be given up for the Beloved. Renunciation will acquire breadth and depth, eating at the very roots of self. Little by little God will try the soul, moving from renunciation to renunciation, and these of an ever more interior and purifying nature: stripping it of natural inclinations and aversions, of the good opinion it may have of itself, or any self-conceived perfection, goodness or spirituality; or even of the perception of its own progress. One by one these tags by which the soul clings to tangible support are taken away. Thus, progress in the interior way is a progress by losses. This is God's method of "re-forming" the supernatural character; and the soul, by its co-operation, by its submission and consent to the purifying action of God, undergoes in this manner a more passive asceticism than that ordinarily practiced outside the mystical life.

Surely Our Lord gently invites loved ones to a generous surrender of themselves to Him, a surrender of all their ideas, preferences, likes and dislikes, petty ambitions, self-seeking of every kind, that He may be All in All to them in loving union. "Seek, and you shall find," He says; "knock, and it shall be opened to you."* When we have knocked, by earnest, persevering effort at prayer, by holy desires, self-denial and the like, there remains only the willing submission to the touch of God's Hand as it

* Matt. 7:7.

works the more passive and penetrating purifications. But, as has been so aptly remarked, most people "do not progress much beyond a well-directed cultivation of self for God. They build up their character admirably, but it is *their* character. They will not lose all, including self, to find All; and so they remain in the middle passage."*

Such a losing of self is a most happy loss – resulting only in a finding of self again in the Beloved, with Whom it becomes one mind, one will, one loving heart. So, too, thought the lovers in the poem which the Abbé Brémond quotes in *Prayer and Poetry*:

> The lover knocks at the door of the Beloved, and a voice replies from within: "Who is there?" "It is I," he said, and the voice replied: "There is no room for thee and me in this house." And the door remained shut. Then the lover returned to the desert, and fasted and prayed in solitude. After a year he came back, and knocked once more at the door. Once more the voice asked: "Who is there?" He replied: "It is thyself." And the door opened to him.

It is ordinary contemplation and mystic prayer that gives the facility for such wholehearted surrender of self. To the will it communicates inclination and strength to do whatever the Beloved requires; to the mind, light to know there is nothing safer, better, sweeter, than the utter, irrevocable gift of self to that Holy and Ineffable Being Who has made the weak creature worthy to share the lot of the saints in light.

---

* Howley, op. cit., p. 274.

CHAPTER XIV

VISIONS, VOICES AND MYSTIC PRAYER

The tendency to confuse visions and revelations with mystic prayer is (it may be hoped) constantly diminishing. It may still linger where there has been no trouble taken to investigate the true character of mysticism. Visions and locutions are phenomena which, most probably, never make their appearance in the lives of the greater number of people enjoying contemplative prayer. In themselves they may not be uncommon. To meet with seers and prophets, or at least with people who have met them, is more usual than might be supposed. The writer has known individuals claiming to be recipients of visions or revelations. One at least gave no sign of possessing a grace of contemplative prayer and could scarcely be called a mystic.

Again, very good persons, and some even destined for high sanctity, have beheld apparitions and heard voices outside of mystic prayer. St. Joan of Arc was guided by voices which seemingly came to her apart from prayer. These voices speaking to her from the other world were the inspiration of her mission and they directed her infallibly, as they were from God. Nothing is mentioned in her life about mystical prayer and union – though presumably she had it. So with St. Bernadette. She beheld the Queen of Heaven many times in external visions; yet there is no indication of mystic prayer in connection with these appearances, though she was absorbed by them to such an extent as to be insensible of what was happening around her. There is thus no necessary connection between visions, voices and mystic prayer.

Mystic prayer is obscure, intangible, indistinct, without image, form or figure, and has no intrinsic affinity for visions or revelations. The visionary can describe his experience in particular and definite image and language; the mystic cannot. Whatever is definite, clearly seen, and able to be apprehended in form or figure, comes through the channels of sense and is therefore non-mystic and purely accessory.

Of course many of the greatest saints and mystics had these unusual experiences. Frequently, indeed, these have tended to obscure the thing of real interest and value in their lives – their prayer. How often we hear about St. Margaret Mary's visions of the Sacred Heart; how seldom about the long hours she spent in loving repose before God – repose which was her true life, her main occupation, her mystic prayer.

In the case of so many who have been subject to extraordinary phenomena, there have been contradictions, non-fulfillment of prophetic utterances, misinterpretations, even disedification of life. This fact, together with a mistaken tendency to label these persons mystics when perhaps they have never experienced the mystic union, is at least partly accountable for any distaste or distrust associated with the word and subject of mysticism.

The frequent deception in regard to visions and voices, or their meaning, has made even saints wonder on occasion whether these experiences were from God, self or devil. And they have more than once erred in interpretation; it is so easy to intrude one's own spirit. Furthermore, these things possess no great efficacy or power in themselves to sanctify and deepen the soul's union with God, nor can they in any manner be truly like unto Him. So the wise soul loses no time in so much as even testing the spirits to see whether or not they are of God, but passes on direct to God, Who is apprehended only in that general, indistinct, indescribable, obscure, loving knowledge which is far more sanctifying than extraordinary and incidental phenomena. When we have this, we have God. And we cannot be deceived – as in visions and voices – for the mystic union can come neither from self nor from evil spirit, which uses sense operations, but only from God; and it takes place in the inner chamber of the soul where sense cannot penetrate nor the devil enter in but where the Divine Guest alone dwells.

CHAPTER XV

SYSTEM OF ST. JOHN OF THE CROSS

In the exposition of contemplative and mystic prayer, its nature and characteristics, there has been no greater master than St. John of the Cross. To read his works, brief though they are, is to be amazed at his vast knowledge of the mystical life in all its phases. Though he has much in his writings that can best be understood and relished by saints, the greater portion of his work is dedicated to the aid of beginners in contemplative and mystic prayer. And in this line he has no equal. Someone has called him the world's foremost psychologist. He not only knows the human soul but he has imparted a unique quality to all his pages – a breathing in them, as it were, of the Holy Spirit of Love.

St. John of the Cross pictures the spiritual life as a journey of the soul to divine union. This journey he calls night – and for three reasons:

The first is derived from the point from which the soul sets out, the privation of the desire of all pleasure in all the things of this world, by detachment therefrom. This is as night for every desire and sense of man. The second, from the road by which it travels; that is, faith, for faith is obscure, like night, to the understanding. The third, from the goal to which it tends, God, incomprehensible and infinite, Who in this life is as night to the soul.*

In the beginning the soul makes use of what is at hand to lead it to God, such as the visible things of His creation. By meditation on the beauties and wonders of created things, the mind is lifted up to the Creator of them. Especially does the heart dilate at the marvels and goodness of His supernatural creation, the mysteries of the Incarnation and Redemption, and of the Church, the very Bride of Christ.

But these are created reflections of His splendor; traces, vestiges, shadows of His ineffable Being that cannot be seen in this life. They elevate mind and heart to Him. But a creature, bearing no proportion to the Divine Essence, cannot serve as proximate means of union with Him Whose Infinite Nature is darkness to the understanding and cannot be represented as It is in Itself by any finite form or figure.

The soul therefore, that will ascend in this life to the supreme good and rest must pass beyond all these steps of considerations, form and notions, because they bear no likeness or proportion to the end, which is God, toward which it tends.†

The proximate means of union of the soul with God must therefore be of a spiritual nature, and that means is faith. For the union of spirit with Spirit is not wrought by sense but by that which is above sense, namely, faith. Our entire life in this world, insofar as it is deprived of the clear vision of God, is a life of faith. And the journey of the soul toward God is a journey in faith, obscure and dark, like night both to the senses and to the understanding.

As to prayer itself, it first becomes a prayer of faith when the senses can no longer be used as a way of approach to God; that is, when meditation becomes impossible and the soul is led by grace to seek Him beyond images, ideas, thoughts and feelings

* *The Ascent of Mount Carmel,* Bk. I, chap. 2.
† Ibid., Bk. II, chap. 12.

– in a simple propension of love toward God. This transitional period of prayer is called the night of the senses, for the senses are deprived of all pleasure in things and are thus in darkness with regard to them.

With this grace the soul co-operates by self-denial and detachment from all things. The detachment and mortification of sense must be thoroughgoing, and consists in suppressing desire and avoiding pleasure. Thereby the soul is left free to commune with God in the way of the spirit, in faith, which is dark and dry to sense.

> It is supreme ignorance for anyone to think he can ever attain to the high state of union with God before he casts away from him the desire for natural things, and of supernatural also, so far as it concerns self-love. "Every one of you that does not renounce all that he possesses cannot be My disciple."*

This laboring at the mortification of the desires is the active side of the night of sense, being that which the soul of itself can do. The passive side is, the being open to God's work, the infused prayer. This prayer is wrought by a spiritual impression which occupies the mind and heart in a loving attention to God. In the beginning it is confusion and suffering because of the distress and helplessness of the senses. But in time the soul becomes accustomed to the new prayer of faith, which gradually takes possession of the whole life.

During this first "night" the five external senses are mortified, and the desires are purified so that the lower nature is brought into subjection to the higher. In a superb chapter on the doctrine of renunciation as implied in the Gospel, St. John of the Cross stresses the necessity for the practice of genuine self-denial. Some excerpts follow:

> Would that I could persuade spiritual persons that the way of God consisteth not in the multiplicity of meditations, ways of devotion or sweetness, though these may be necessary

---

* Ibid., Bk. I, chap. 5, 2.

for beginners, but in one necessary thing only, in knowing how to deny themselves in earnest, inwardly and outwardly, giving themselves up to suffer for Christ's sake, and annihilating themselves utterly. He who shall exercise himself herein, will then find all this and much more. And if he be deficient at all in this exercise, which is the sum and root of all virtue, all he may do will be but beating the air; utterly profitless, notwithstanding great meditations and communications. That spirituality, therefore, that would travel in sweetness at its own ease, shunning the following of Christ is, in my opinion, nothing worth.*

Without this self-denial, real advance in the way of perfection and divine union cannot be made. One must lose the desire for anything that is not simply God or the expression of His will. Moreover, certain habits of voluntary imperfection impede the progress of the soul:

These habitual imperfections are, for instance, much talking, certain attachments which we never resolve to break through – such as to individuals, to a book or a cell, to a particular food, to certain society, the satisfaction of one's taste, science, news and such things. Every one of these, if the soul is attached and habituated to them, retards growth and progress in goodness.†

The strength for such detachment comes from prayer. This simple mystic prayer is the dynamic center communicating great energy to the will. At first it may be very arid and distasteful, but its great power is soon felt in correcting the wayward inclinations of sense and in nourishing growth in virtue. The soul, however, must be generous in its co-operation, in following the workings of grace. And strangely enough, it is not the mortification of the desires that causes grief and aridity in the soul. On the contrary, it is indulgence and gratification that bring dryness, misery, fatigue and weariness, for the desires are

*   Ibid., Bk. II, chap. 7.
†   Ibid.

like little children who are never satisfied but are ever crying out for more:

> He who does not repress the satisfaction of his appetites will never enjoy the ordinary tranquillity of rejoicing in God, through the instrumentality of His creatures... He who is spiritually minded must be wholly tending toward God, for all his actions and affections are those of the spiritual life. Such a one finds in all things that knowledge of God which is delicious, sweet, chaste, pure, spiritual, joyous and loving.*

Mortification of all the desires brings peace, calm and recollection, wherein the soul can hear the voice of God in spiritual prayer and advance unhindered in the delights of spiritual union:

> Oh, would that spiritual persons knew how they are losing the good things of the spirit, abundantly furnished, because they will not raise up their desires above trifles, and how they might have the sweetness of all things in the pure food of the spirit if they would only forgo them.†

As the soul becomes established in its spiritual way of communing with God, He leads it more and more along the path of renunciation. The divine love communicated to the soul by infused prayer strips it increasingly of the roots of self-love. One thing after another falls away from it. This or that possession or attachment, cherished notion, opinion, taste or inclination, which hitherto the soul fondled dearly as its own, is relinquished – and indeed, without effort. The soul, it seems, cannot help itself, for the riches of that general, obscure, loving knowledge which it experiences, of necessity loose the strings of attachment to all else. "The soul is now detached not only from all outward things but even from itself: it is, as it were, undone, assumed by, and dissolved in love."‡

* Ibid., Bk. III, chap. 25.
† Ibid., Bk. I, chap. 5, 4.
‡ *Spiritual Canticle,* XXIV, 14.

Those whom God designs to bring to yet higher union with Him He casts into the night of the spirit. This night overtakes the soul while it is still lingering in the first night, that of sense. The soul is plunged into a drastic purging process of darkness, pain and abandonment. The positive element and cause of this painful night is, of course, the infused contemplation. The deep impression of divine grace, from its very brilliance, blinds the soul so that it seems to be enveloped in a thick darkness. Yet at the same time it so illumines the soul as to reveal the hidden miseries of self which had not been removed by the first purification in the night of sense but have remained in the soul like old stains in a garment.

This is truly a severe trial and crucifixion, but the soul is safe in the darkness. By its utter helplessness it is forced to cast all its care upon God in complete abandonment, walking not by what it can see, feel or know, but by pure faith. Such purifying contemplation is the source of inestimable blessings:

> O souls that seek your own ease and comfort, if you knew how necessary for this high state is suffering, and how profitable suffering and mortification are for attaining to these great blessings, you would never seek for comfort anywhere, but you would rather take up the cross with the vinegar and the gall, and you would count it an inestimable favor, knowing that by thus dying to yourselves and to the world, you would live to God in spiritual joy.[*]

The powers of the soul – intellect, memory and will – are purified in this night and brought to God in the operation of the theological virtues of faith, hope and charity. Faith detaches the intellect from natural and supernatural apprehensions, exterior and interior. Anything that is distinct and clear to the understanding, represented in image form or figure, is rejected, as being in no way proportionate to the Being of God and therefore ineffectual as proximate means of union with God. Even supernatural or preternatural apprehensions, such as

---

[*] *The Living Flame*, II, 30.

visions and voices and revelations, are to be set aside. The soul must pass beyond them, must be guided past all these particular forms and figures, to rest only in the confused and general loving knowledge which is given in pure contemplation and wrought through spiritual impressions apprehended in the obscurity of faith.

Similarly, the memory is purified and detached from all recollections of these images and forms of particular knowledge, natural and supernatural, so that in the virtue of hope it becomes accustomed to have in mind the "eternal years," looking ever forward to the good things to come. This liberates the memory during prayer, for contemplation is not then obstructed by distractions and reflections of sense or any particular knowledge, but is disposed to abstraction and holy oblivion – which is the proper disposition for receiving the spiritual knowledge God is giving it.

Finally, the will is cleansed in charity, which detaches it from all that is not God. It strips it of all joy in material and temporal things, even such as would be caused by images, statues, pictures of saints, solemn ceremonies, richly decorated chapels, the hearing or preaching of sermons, insofar as these offer the will a merely natural satisfaction to which it might cling. The dark night of the spirit deprives the soul of all this, cutting at the deepest roots of self-love and preparing in the soul that delicacy of spiritual refinement and simplicity necessary for union with God. For this intimate union

the soul's love must be such that it cannot rest on any joy, nor drink of this world's honor and glory, nor recreate itself with any temporal consolation, nor shelter itself in the shade of created help and protection: it must repose nowhere; it must avoid the society of all its inclinations, mourn its loneliness, until it shall find the Bridegroom to its perfect contentment.*

* *Spiritual Canticle*, XXXIV.

Few, perhaps, come so far along the spiritual path, and these moreover vary in degree of perfection, according to the depth of union and divine charity willed by God. But when the process of purification matures, darkness yields to the approaching dawn, light and joy take possession, and the soul dwells in peace, in a calm and sweet atmosphere of love which never leaves it, for it has become one with its Bridegroom in the union of love, wherein "the soul burns away sweetly in God."*

St. John of the Cross goes on to sing in glowing terms of the delights and wonders God now works in the soul, granting it unspeakable favors of grace, virtue and happiness. Let us note, for example, the comment on the line "Thou awakest in my bosom":

> It is utterly impossible to describe what the soul in this awakening knows and feels of the Majesty of God, in the inmost depths of its being. For in the soul resounds an infinite power, with the voice of a multitude of perfections, of thousands and thousands of virtues, wherein itself abiding and subsisting, becomes "terrible as an army set in array," sweet and gracious in Him Who comprehends in Himself all the sweetness and all the graces of His creation.†

Yet with all these marvels of grace and union, with all this exquisite joy refreshing it, the soul still remains in the sphere of obscure contemplation. Since the barrier of this mortal life is not passed, the soul is ever within the domain of faith – until the dazzling light of the Beatific Vision breaks upon it in the life of the world to come. Thus

> contemplation is called night, because it is dim; and that is the reason it is called mystical theology – that is, secret or hidden wisdom of God, where without the sound of words, or the intervention of any bodily or spiritual sense, as it were in silence and repose, in the darkness of sense and nature,

---

* *The Dark Night of the Soul,* Bk. II.
† *The Living Flame,* IV, 9.

God teaches the soul – and the soul knows not how – in a most secret and hidden way.*

This is the highest state of the soul's spiritual journey in this life. Contemplative prayer is its secret, its source, its development and fruition. And the blessings and happiness of this state should encourage the soul to pursue its prayer so that, if God so pleases, He may grant it at least the beginnings of contemplation – which indeed is not uncommon. All that has been treated of in these pages is this initial mystic and simple prayer which, if the soul corresponds to it faithfully, will increase in power and depth according to the election of the Divine Spouse.

May this infinitely good and holy God, Who desires so lovingly to be the Bridegroom of human souls, lead us all securely and happily through the night of faith of this life even to the vision, power and glory of the world to come!

---

* *Spiritual Canticle*, XXXIX, 12.

APPENDIX

The teaching of an "acquired" contemplation, a kind of compromise or go-between bridging meditation and mystic prayer, augmented the error of quietism. This so-called "acquired" contemplation was held to be non-mystic and therefore the result of mere human effort. It will be interesting and instructive to consider a few points admirably discussed by Howley in his *Psychology and Mystical Experience*.

He observes that the development of quietism in the seventeenth century was due to an attempted systematizing of contemplative prayer as meditation had been systematized:

The complex method of meditation had finally come to be advocated as the one and only type of mental prayer suitable for all. Other types of mental prayer, less discursive, more unitive and affective, were discouraged by the propagandists of meditation. The broad result of this was that the meditation became the normal form of mental prayer throughout the religious orders and the devout laity. Even in the Carmels and the Visitations of France, the natural homes of contemplative prayer, the meditation type drove out more unitive forms. Mental prayer became standardized and uniform, to the no small comfort of spiritual directors.[*]

Of course a reaction set in. There were then, as there are now and will be at all times,

devout persons who did not relish the meditation and preferred some form of contemplative prayer, such as had been largely popularized by the early members of the Visitation,

[*]   Chapter on "Quietism."

who had been trained in the spiritual life by St. Francis de Sales and St. Jeanne de Chantal.*

People both lay and religious were found using a prayer that had none of the complexity of the meditation, being quite simple and free of discursiveness. Yet nothing extraordinary was seen to happen. There were no ecstasies and raptures, no colorful visions nor tales of prophecy. Consequently, to give a name to this prayer some theologians invented the "acquired" contemplation. But, as Howley goes on to say:

> This contributed more than anything else to the development of quietistic doctrine, for Molinos and his followers pushed the methods recognized as legitimate in the so-called acquired contemplation to extremes. It is not to be found in the earlier mystics, as Saudreau and others have shown, unless violence is done to the text. The new category became classic, and the possibility and frequency of the non-mystical contemplation was an accepted commonplace with spiritual writers until our present times.†

Today, however, that teaching is seriously and energetically questioned. Psychology shows a strong presumption against it, and theologians and spiritual writers adhere more closely to the texts of the great masters and teachers of prayer, the mystics themselves. In other words, the prayer of simplicity is mystic, a common mystic prayer, and is reached only through the night of the senses, as explained by St. John of the Cross. It cannot, moreover, be systematized, but develops with the liberty of the Holy Spirit.

*   Ibid.
†   Ibid.

BIBLIOGRAPHY

Baker, A., *Sancta Sophia [Holy Wisdom]*, London, Burns, Oates and Washbourne. An older work but one of the best in English on prayer and mortification.

Barbanson, C., O. F. M. Cap., *The Secret Paths of Divine Love*, London, Burns, Oates and Washbourne, 1928.

Brémond, Henri, *A Literary History of Religious Thought in France;* three first volumes in English, New York, Macmillan. The second volume deals specifically with the mystics. There are choice selections descriptive of contemplative prayer.

Browne, Henry, S. J., *Darkness or Light*, St. Louis, Herder, 1925. Academic and controversial.

Butler, Cuthbert, O. S. B., *Western Mysticism*, New York, Dutton, 1924.

Chapman, John, O. S. B., *Spiritual Letters*, London, Sheed and Ward, 1937. This, the most enlightening and common-sense book on matters of prayer that has appeared in years, consists mainly of letters of direction.

De Besse, Ludovic, O. F. M. Cap., *The Science of Prayer*, Benziger, 1925, 189 pages. A clear-cut description of the progress of prayer, as well as of ordinary mystic prayer, which the author designates the "prayer of faith."

De Caussade, J. P., S. J., *Abandonment to Divine Providence*, St. Louis, Herder, 1921. Excellent in its treatment of the passive trials and purifications, with especially valuable letters of direction to those in the way of spiritual prayer. This work will be greatly relished by interior souls on account of the accurate portrayal of their state. *Progress in Prayer*, Herder, 1904, 178 pages. Practical advice for clearing away hindrances to contemplation.

Dobbins, Dunstan, O. F. M. Cap., *Franciscan Mysticism*, New York, Wagner, 1927.
They That Are Christ's, Dublin, Brown and Nolan.

Francis de Sales, St., *Treatise on the Love of God*, Newman Bookshop, 1942, 555 pages.

Garrigou-Lagrange, Reginald, O. P., *Christian Perfection and Contemplation according to St. Thomas and St. John of the Cross*, Herder, 1937, 470 pages.

Grou, Jean Nicholas, S. J., *Manual for Interior Souls*, London, St. Anselm's Society, 1889. Very fine for those in the contemplative way, with lucid explanations of the principle of interior prayer and its action on general behavior.

Howley, J., *Psychology and Mystical Experience*, England, Sands (Herder), 1920. Contains a splendid analysis of the act of contemplation from the viewpoint of psychology; also a penetrating treatment of Quietism.

James, Father, O. F. M. Cap., *The Franciscan Vision*, London, Burns, Oates and Washbourne, 1937.

John of the Cross, St., *Complete Works*, translated and edited by E. Allison Peers, Burns, Oates and Washbourne, 1934-1935, 3 volumes. Makes the great Spanish mystic available to the modern reader. (The older translation of Lewis, which the author prefers as more accurate and more pleasing in style, has been used in the present text.) *The Ascent of Mount Carmel* is of the greatest value to the student and director.

Knowles, David, O. S. B., *Studies in the English Mystics*, London, Burns, Oates and Washbourne, 1927.

Leen, Edward, C. S. Sp., *Progress Through Mental Prayer*, Sheed and Ward, 1935, 276 pages.

Poulain, Auguste, S. J., *The Graces of Interior Prayer*, translated by Leonora L. Yorke-Smith, Herder, 1910, 637 pages. Helpful for directors of souls, and abounding in quotations from the mystics. This author holds the doctrine of "acquired" contemplation; his treatment of the prayer of simplicity is consequently misleading, tending to introduce the soul prematurely to contemplative prayer.

Saudreau, A., *The Mystical State*, Benziger, 1924. Holds the wide accessibility of contemplation.

The Degrees of the Spiritual Life, Benziger, 1907, 2 volumes. Volume two treats of contemplative prayer.

Tanquerey, Adolphe, S. S., *The Spiritual Life,* Tournai, Society of St. John the Evangelist, Desclée et Cie, 1932, 750 pages. This treatise on ascetical and mystical theology constitutes the most complete and up-to-date manual in English.

Teresa, St., *Life,* written by herself, Newman Bookshop, 1943, 516 pages.

The Way of Perfection, London, T. Baker, 1935, 272 pages.

Watkin, E. I., *The Philosophy of Mysticism,* New York, Harcourt, Brace, 1920. Gives the philosophical basis for mysticism.

The Bow in the Clouds, New York, Macmillan, 1932.

Williams, W., *The Mysticism of St. Bernard of Clairvaux,* London, Burns, Oates and Washbourne, 1931.

Williamson, B. *Supernatural Mysticism,* St. Louis, Herder, 1921.

Ingram Content Group UK Ltd.
Milton Keynes UK
UKHW022132030423
419589UK00014B/1005

9 781088 038475